Specifically To Youth

Specifically To Youth

A BOOK OF SERMONS

by

Harry H. Kruener

**DEAN OF THE CHAPEL,
DENISON UNIVERSITY**

HARPER & BROTHERS   PUBLISHERS   NEW YORK

Grateful acknowledgment is made to the following publishers for permission
to quote material from their books:

Henry Holt and Company, Inc., for the lines from "The Road Not Taken" from
Collected Poems of Robert Frost, copyright 1943 by Henry Holt and Company.
Random House, Inc., New York, and Faber & Faber, Ltd., London, for the lines
from "September 1, 1939" by W. H. Auden from *Collected Poetry,* copyright
1943 by Random House.
Dodd, Mead & Company, New York, and Burns, Oates & Washbourne, Ltd.,
London, for the lines from "The Hound of Heaven" from *Selected Poems of
Francis Thompson.*
Harcourt, Brace & Company, Inc., and Faber & Faber, Ltd., London, for the lines
from "The Rock" by T. S. Eliot from *Collected Poems 1909–1935,* copyright
1936 by Harcourt, Brace & Company.

Library of Congress catalog card number: 59-7152

CONTENTS

FOREWORD

ALL of these sermons were first preached at Denison University. As the Dean of the Chapel there for the past four years, it has been my duty, at once perilous and delightful, to stand before one thousand young men and women each Thursday evening to try to interpret the Christian Faith. These sermons were part of services of worship in which the students participated and it is hard for me to think of them otherwise. Congregations make sermons. I have been fortunate to have an intelligent and attentive congregation.

The sermons that seemed to survive best at Denison were used in many other university chapels. They were frequently preached in churches as well, churches of every size and denominational persuasion. While some adaptation was needed on such occasions, I have been surprised how little was required. This leads me to observe that speaking "specifically to youth" may not be as specific or peculiar as we often presume.

Of course, a college audience represents only one band of the full spectrum of the "threescore years and ten" seen in the churches, but it has its own life. It laughs in a different way, it grows hushed and tense, it hangs on to an argument longer, it enjoys a thrust at its own expense. You can use the most subtle illustration, the most out-of-the-way reference, and get away with it. You can expect lots of surprises. But when all is said and done, what impresses a college preacher week after week is how common are our human ills, how much each of us, at twenty or at fifty, reflects the troubles and hopes of our times, and how we all look, with mixed but honest hearts, for some answer from our Faith. I'm convinced there is no Gospel addressed solely to youth. There is only one Gospel, and the best preacher to students is he who consistently forgets how young they are.

Here, then, is how one man tries to speak to a particular situation, but beyond that situation to the younger generation of America, and all who dare to share its life and thought. The first group of sermons in this book is theological. Since in our Chapel we are overwhelmingly Protestant with no large fundamentalist right or humanist left, I undoubtedly go "down the middle" in interpreting Christianity. I hope I do this without being colorless or unfair. The second section deals with personal problems. They are universal: the "Organization Man," for instance, is simply the "Big Wheel" on campus. The third section moves right into the dormitory and into those hardy perennials of the bull-session, sex, drink, war, and interfaith marriages.

I appreciate more than I can say the work of my secretaries, Helen Dunfield and Adra Yard, in preparing the manuscript. I want to thank the staff of Harper & Brothers for patiently helping me shape for print my preacher's all-too-oral style and colloquialisms. Permissions for the quotations used have been graciously given as acknowledged. The author is grateful to the Whittemore Associates and to the publishers of *The Intercollegian* and *The Pulpit* for permission to reprint material which originally appeared in somewhat different form in their publications.

This book is dedicated to my wife, Martha, whose love is only equaled by her courage to live.

HARRY H. KRUENER

Lent, 1959
Granville, Ohio

I.

INTERPRETING THE CHRISTIAN FAITH

ONE

A Religion of the Eye or Ear

ONE of the most fascinating things about Western civilization is the creative mixture it presents of two cultures, that of the Jew and that of the Greek. If you want to understand modern London or modern New York or Paris, you had better understand ancient Jerusalem and Athens. These two ways of life over the centuries have curiously blended and become our way of life. At times they mix, and at times they separate, something like oil and vinegar in the cruet on the dining-room table, but they are always there.

This uneasy mixture is particularly apparent in religion. Martin Buber, one of the greatest living Jewish scholars, describes it by saying: "The Hebrew is more the ear-man, while the Greek is more the eye-man. The Hebrew is more motor-being, while the Greek is visual-being. The Hebrew lives in time, with a sense of history, the Greek lives more in space. The Hebrew did not so much see God—he said no man can see God, but he did hear God's voice. The fundamental prayer of the Jew is 'Hear, O Israel.'" The Greek had a religion of the eye; all you did was look at and contemplate God. The Hebrew had a religion of the ear; God spoke and you had to respond and answer.

This distinction is suggestive not only for history; it's a valid distinction for us today. We have those among us who have a religion of the eye. We like to look at religion, at Christianity, but nothing more. We are spectators—thoughtful and reverent spectators, but spectators none the less. Irvin S. Cobb once said: "In politics I'm a democrat; in religion an innocent bystander." Good, there's nothing too wrong with that: Christianity is something to look at. But there are also some among us who have a religion of the ear. We can't stand on the side looking at God. God is speaking, calling our name, and we have to answer. Religion, in other words, is always conversation. We can't be bystanders, we can't be spectators, we can't stay out of it. Christianity, if it's anything, is something to which you must respond and commit yourself. Christianity is a call to which you must answer. This is religion of the ear.

There are times, I'm sure, when religion of the eye is the finest religion we can have. Sometimes we sit in church and are glad that no words are spoken. Just to see the Gothic arches receding into the dim distance above us, just to watch the candles flickering on the altar, just to look at the gold filigree of the Cross is quite enough for our souls. Adjacent to the University of Chicago campus, there is a little chapel which seats only fifty people. One tiny soft spotlight falls on the altar. Gorgeous stained glass, window after window, is only a dozen feet up the wall, hanging low over the heads of worshipers like a huge crown of red and blue jewels. The Bible talks about the beauty of holiness, but when I'm in that chapel I believe more in the holiness of beauty. I'm a modern man with the heart of an ancient Greek and words would be out of place. Yes, we all experience the religion of the eye.

But it can't stop there, no religion can, and Christianity least of all. Inevitably religion moves from eye to ear, from mystic vision to a direct demand, from contemplation to choice, decision, commitment. Religion won't always let you be a spectator, an innocent bystander. It won't let you comfortably sit on the fence. Dr. Goodspeed says the word "Christian" is a word of Latin derivation. It means, literally, "partisan of Christ," a member of his party. The contemporary allusion is obvious. We think of the partisans of Tito, or the freedom fighters of the underground in Europe during the World War. The one thing you can say about partisans is that they were never neutral, they never played it safe, they never sat on the fence, they never were spectators to the struggle of their day. No, they threw in their lot, they committed themselves, they heard and followed a leader, come hell or high water. So, the very word "Christian" implies a commitment of life, a decision, a choice. For us quiet contemplation even in the most beautiful chapel in the world is not enough. As Christians we are called to be partisans of Christ. We hear and we answer. Every great religion moves from eye to ear, from vision to demand, from contemplation to an ultimate choice.

I want to ask two questions at this point. First, if Christianity requires decision, then why are some of us afraid to decide, afraid to commit ourselves to Christ? And second, what finally makes us decide to become Christians? or, to phrase this second question differently, What happens to make a bystander into a partisan? What changes our faith from a religion of the eye to a religion of the ear?

First, why do many of us prefer to be bystanders in matters of Christianity, to look at it but never to hear and answer? One very good reason is that *as young people we resist the idea of choice of any sort.* We don't want to close our minds. We want to keep them honestly as open as possible. Any commitment, any decision narrows our lives, and we don't want it. In the springtime of life this is healthy, this is good. You remember Robert Frost in his haunting poem "The Road Not Taken."

> Two roads diverged in a yellow wood
> And sorry I could not travel both
> And be one traveler, long I stood
> And looked down one as far as I could
> To where it bent in the undergrowth;
> Then took the other . . .

He concludes:

> I shall be telling this with a sigh
> Somewhere ages and ages hence:
> Two roads diverged in a wood, and I—

I took the one less traveled by,
And that has made all the difference.[1]

Two roads do come to us, and we peer down one road as far as we can, and we're sorry we cannot travel both, and we stand there long, and even after we go down one road we often think about it with a sigh and wonder about "the road not taken." So, we'll avoid the choice as long as we can. It is natural in youth to feel this way, because the truth is there's death in every choice. You die to one road when you go down the other: there's no getting away from it. You choose to be a lawyer and you can't be a doctor, you choose to marry one girl and not another; you choose to major in the arts and you can't in the sciences. And always there comes back the haunting feeling about "the road not taken," what would have happened if I had gone that other way? No, you're right to be afraid of choice because there's a bit of death in every choice. You die to one way of life in order to live to another, and youth wants both. We hate choice; we're honestly afraid of becoming partisan of anything, of anybody.

Now all Christianity can ever say is that, good and healthy as your fear may be, you can't stand forever at the fork of the road. Life has a nasty way of making you choose. Neutrality is the one thing that life never allows. You may try to be neutral in politics for a while, but the ballot has a way of confronting you, and there it is, yes or no. You may try to be objective about the race issue, but some day the issue comes up in your club, your fraternity, and you either drop in the blackball or you don't. And you can shout at life, "Confound you, why did you make me choose, I'm an easygoing decent sort of chap, I never hurt anybody, why did you have to butt in here?" But it's there and you've got to stand up and be counted; the eyes of a million men may be on you. You may wish you could be neutral about a war, but a gun is put in your hand and you usually do something with it. So in religion, some-day the blunt question comes up: "Is Jesus Christ the clue to the meaning of life or isn't he?" and we line up with those who

[1] Robert Frost, *Collected Poems of Robert Frost* (New York: Henry Holt & Co., 1939).

believe or those who do not. Yes, whether you like it or not, life will someday make you a partisan. You will choose.

Some of us, then, prefer to be bystanders in religion because we resist the idea of choice of any sort. And some of us are prevented from becoming partisans of Christ *because of the theology that seems to go with it.* Jesus himself is attractive enough, but all those theories about him are a nuisance—the Son of God, the Virgin Birth, "He saves us from sin," "He rose from the dead." We honestly say: "If to become a partisan of Christ I have to swallow all those theories about him, then you can count me out."

Now we can all sympathize with such theological bystanders. The facts of Jesus are one thing: the simple life of Christ. But the theories about those facts always seem to complicate it. "I'll stick to the facts, no theories," we like to say. But really does that make sense, speaking practically? Is there any fact in history, any person, any event, that—sooner or later—doesn't develop a theory, an interpretation, around it? And in the long run may not the theory be as important as the fact itself? There's the hydrogen bomb, for instance. The fact is simple: a plane flies over a tropical island and drops a bomb which generates heat, radioactivity, what have you. But let me ask: "When the first hydrogen bomb was dropped did you just ask or think about the fact?" No, you thought much more than that if you thought at all: What is the nature of man that he of all God's creatures should plot his own suicide? Will the human race be exterminated; will this old globe that has produced so much of beauty and love become some day soon a burnt-over star floating lonely in space? What is the destiny of man, is this the sad end of the human adventure? These are theories, you see, interpretations of facts in history, theologies if you please. And you and I are living in a world in which theories about facts are often as worrisome as the facts themselves. So of Jesus Christ: you can't have him come into history, shattering like a bomb the horizons of time, without some theories about him, without Christian theology. Don't be a bystander, then, purely because of a fear of theology. You don't want a fixed theology. You don't want a theology handed down to you. But you should have some theology, if only because you are a person who thinks, and thinks hard, about God.

We could go on. Still others are kept from becoming committed Christians *because of the Church.* Most young people express it by saying: "The Church is full of hypocrites. I simply can't take it."

Now, of course, there are hypocrites in the Church as in any other human institution. The person who is always talking about hypocrites is apt to be an idealist—a disappointed idealist, but an idealist none the less. Consequently, he's got the wrong definition of the Church. The Church is not a society of saints, as he thinks it is; it's a society of sinners who know the grace of God. In other words, the Church is the only society whose one requirement for membership is that we should be unworthy of membership. All this, bystanders should honestly recognize. The Church has no monopoly of hypocrites.

What keeps people, then, from decision in matters of Christianity? First, the fear of choice of any sort, then Christian theology (or what they think is Christian theology), then the Church itself.

But let me go on to the other question: What finally makes people decide, what makes them out-and-out partisans of Jesus Christ, what makes them Christians? Here I can only state my personal faith. I believe that most of us decide for Christ when we acknowledge a sense of need. We can call it a sense of sin, we can define it any number of ways, but all I want to say to you is that this need is there in any committed Christian. It's like Lillian Roth's story in her motion picture *I'll Cry Tomorrow.* At a certain point she had to say, "I'm an alcoholic and I need help," before she could overcome her weakness. So there is a raw honesty about a Christian. There's a pain in the soul that won't be healed with the thousand cheap aspirins the world offers. At a certain point he says to himself: "When all the polish is off and I've seen through all the nice things people say about me, down at the center I'm a sinner and I need God." He has a deep sense of need.

I believe most of us decide for Christ when we take a step of faith. The Christian is a gambler; the bystander never is. The bystander is obsessed with security and for that reason he is never secure. The Christian knows that there is no security in this world except the love of God. He bets his life on that, he takes a long chance. You can't be a Christian without a bit of the heroic in your soul. The most rational man is the man who knows the limits of reason. He lives by faith.

I believe something further, that no man can tell us when or how to make our decisions in matters of religion. We have our "Hours of Decision" on radio and television, I know. We have our ministers who point long fingers at us and say: "Now you must accept Christ, now you must decide." But no man can tell another man when his hour of crisis is come. No man can tell another man how the glory of God may come to his soul. The Greeks, you recall, had two words for time. One was *chronos,* which means clock time, measured time, ticking off into hours, days, months, and years. But the other word was *kairos,* which means, literally, high-time, time of fulfillment, of decision. And you can always tell another man his *chronos,* his clock time. But you can never tell another man his *kairos,* his high-time before God, high-time of decision in the things of the spirit. That is each man's deepest secret.

Finally I believe—and in some ways I hesitate to say it—that a real decision to be a Christian is the most significant decision you'll ever make in this mortal life. I wish I could let you "off the hook" more easily than that; I wish I could let myself off. But I remember what a sixteenth-century British sailor once said. He had sailed all his life with Sir Francis Drake. When he came back home someone ridiculed him: "You haven't got much to show for all those years, have you?" "No," he said, "I haven't much. I've been cold, hungry, desperately frightened often enough in life—even shipwrecked. But I'm sure of one thing: I've been with the greatest captain that ever sailed the seas."

Well, there it is. As a Christian I'm sure I'm no better man than countless others. But I've known a bit of the cold and the dark fright of the sea and I'm not ashamed of my Captain. This is my commitment. This is religion of the ear.

TWO

On Sin

ANDRE GIDE, the French novelist, in his lovely short
story "The Pastoral Symphony" tells of a young girl, Gertrude,
who has been blind from birth. Her blindness really protected her,
so that she had a childlike, sentimental picture of people around
her, which neither her friends nor family tried to upset. Then one
day an operation was performed on her eyes so that she could see.
Two things immediately struck her with crushing meaning. One
was that nature was more beautiful than she had ever imagined it
would be, light and color and form in space. The other was that
the faces of men were sadder than she ever imagined they would
be: lined with care, with inner anxiety and restlessness. She almost
wished that her eyes had never been opened.

My subject is really on that sad aspect of men's faces. I want us
to think about the Christian's sense of sin. And here I might as
well admit that this is not a pleasant sermon; you won't like it. A
university such as mine seems to be one place where you don't talk
about sin. Or, if you do, you whisper it or make it quite harmless.
"After all," said one dear lady in my town, "why talk about sin to
so many nice people?" And you recall the midwestern college
catalogue that advertised to the parents that its campus was located
"seven miles from any known form of sin." There it is, we are the

"nice people." Sin is out there, a comfortable distance away, something other people do in other places, the people who are not nice.

But if a university keeps quiet about sin, our world talks about
it much more than it did twenty years ago. We're willing to admit
that modern man has a very sad face. W. H. Auden, the poet,
speaks of our age as knowing "the distance of God" more than any
other. That's a good definition of sin: "the distance of God."
Robert Oppenheimer, watching the first atomic explosion, speaks
of physicists having known a sense of sin, which "no vulgarity, no
humor can erase." In T. S. Eliot's *The Cocktail Party* everyone sits
around to find out how Sir Harcourt-Reilly, a psychiatrist, will
wrestle with the problem of sin. In no flippant manner he says to
his patient: "Your business is not to clear your conscience, but to
learn how to bear the burdens on your conscience." We might as
well face it. There's something about modern life that makes most
of us, if we're sensitive at all, take seriously this business of what
the Christian calls sin. We may not like what we see, we may wish
we were blind, but once our eyes are opened, we must admit
modern man has a good deal of sadness in his face.

What, then, does the Christian mean by sin? We might start
with the simple statement that, according to the Christian faith,
every man has a sense of having lost God, some way or other. The
Bible isn't abstract about it; it's just descriptive; it says: "All have
sinned" (Rom. 3:23). This doesn't mean what the world usually
calls sin, some infraction of the moral law. That would be nice;
then one could plan to get seven miles away from sin and feel
quite smug about it. "We're not sinners like other men." No,
when the Gospel talks about sin it's on a deeper level than that.
It's a description of each of us, that deep down we've proved
irresponsive and false to the love of God, betrayed our Creator,
distrusted the Reality behind all reality, and gone our own way as
if there were no God. A girl who was telling me about her broken
love affair said: "It's not what he did; it's that he never once
thought of me." This is the sin behind sins—not what we do but
our basic treason to the Divine Love, our hardness of heart, so that
God can say of each of us: "He never even once thought of me."
And Christianity says that in some way or other every one of us

has made that Great Betrayal. We have lost God. We've got our-selves at the center, not God. We are what Erich Fromm, the psychiatrist, calls "inveterate idolaters."

Now to many people this seems a very pessimistic picture of human nature, and perhaps it is. Compared with many modern theories of man, Christianity always will seem pessimistic and deeply tragic. The other side is that most modern theories are to the Christian quite shallow. There is the glorified-ape theory: man is a complex and interesting animal, "a peeled ape, teetering on his hind legs." And you can say a lot for an ape; he seems to be able to put two and two together rather well; but there's no sense talking about the sin of an ape, even a glorified and complicated one. Man as ape, peeled or unpeeled, has no sense of sin, so far as we know.

There's the escalator theory of man. "Man is progressing on-wards and upwards forever; we're surely better than the cave man; after all, we've got universal education and aspirin and nylon; don't worry about your sins, just step on the escalator of evolu-tionary progress; you're bound to rise." There is no sin in that picture.

Then there's the divine-spark theory. "After all, man is not far from God, he has the divine spark within him. All you need to do is get the bellows out and blow up the spark. Basically we're not sinners, we're just slightly undeveloped saints." At its best this theory is optimistic; at its worst, it's sentimental and naive, like the little boy who wrote an essay on King David: "David was a good and rich king. If there was anything wrong with him it was a slight tendency to adultery." Well, there it is—sin is a slight tendency, a psychological kink, nothing more. We'll work it out somehow.

We also have the thousand and one believers in social utopias. "There's nothing fundamentally wrong with man; the problem isn't sin, it's just better social conditioning. All man needs is better playgrounds, better housing, better environment, better control by the psychologists, better social engineering." The Com-munists fall for this; at the end of the class struggle will come the victory of the proletariat, and then every man will love his neighbor as himself and justice will be won forever. Communism is the playground theory of man writ large.

All of these theories have some marked truth in them; my caricatures are obviously overdone. But Christianity always brands them shallow because they overlook man's basic problem: absolutizing himself, making himself and his works, rather than his Creator, the center. This is the heart of sin, the heart of his alienation, this distance, this lostness, this anxiety—ultimate anxiety—which no one of us can escape. Until they deal with sin—not just with the sense of guilt, but with guilt itself—all theories of man are basically shallow.

The first thing Christianity says, then, is that each of us has a sense of having lost God. "All have sinned." But Christianity goes on to say that *this sense of being lost comes to each of us in different ways*. This inner distance from God, this idolatry, takes many forms, has many symptoms, which we should recognize in ourselves. This is what Jesus talked about. He didn't argue about the lostness of man; he described men who were lost. He told stories, and hearing these stories people said: "That's right, that's just the way I feel before God; he speaks to my condition, my own human situation." Jesus said: "Some men are lost like sheep, some men are lost like coins, some men are lost like the prodigal son, some men are lost like the elder brother who stayed at home and didn't even know he was lost." One of these parables will speak to your condition, will describe your sin, or my sin, or all our sins, says Jesus.

You are lost like a sheep often enough, says Jesus. Down deep you are quite aimless without God. Oh, you are healthy enough. You may even be the life of the party. You may think you're rather tough-minded and practical. But really, all you do from day to day is to nibble the grass one foot in front of your nose, nothing much more. If the grass is green you're happy; if it's brown you baa and bleat at the nature of the universe. But underneath, you're quite aimless, you're lost like a sheep.

This ought not to be hard for us to understand. What is the first symptom of sin, of distance from God? Just plain boredom, purposelessness, meaninglessness. This is a sickness we in the twentieth century are familiar with. We live and die in the "quiet desperation" of a meaningless routine. This is the first "boundary situation" every man faces, according to Tillich—the meaninglessness of it all. Rollo May, the psychoanalyst, tells of a New York bus driver who all his working life had taken the same bus route, down the avenue, crosstown, up the avenue, back crosstown into the garage. One day he couldn't stand it any longer. He went down the avenue and kept going, to Florida. And the strange thing is that when he was brought back for trial all the city—eight million people—rose to his defense! You see, there was a whole city revolting against the meaninglessness of its own daily subway routine, the twentieth-century sickness, boredom.

This is not just the worn-out mood of the old. This is the soft underbelly of all of us which the existentialists are exposing. This is the youth of the Beat Generation. Here is the poet's description of a club on 52nd Street.

> Faces along the bar
> Cling to their average day:
> The lights must never go out,
> The music must always play, . . .
> Lest we should see where we are,
> Lost in a haunted wood,
> Children afraid of the night
> Who have never been happy or good.[1]

I say, we all know something of this first symptom of sin—to be lost in a haunted wood, amazingly afraid to see where we are—to be quite aimless, lost like a sheep.

Again, *you may be lost like a coin,* says Jesus, a coin that has rolled under the carpet and can't be found. In other words, some of us are lost because we are the victim of circumstances, the sin and carelessness of others, the sinful environment, if you please. Sin is not only the wrong we do as individuals; for the Christian it's more tragic than that. Sin is the total predicament in which we humans are often caught, the cobweb of our self-worship and

[1] *Collected Poetry,* W. H. Auden, Random House, New York, 1945. Poem entitled: "September 1, 1939."

faithlessness to God which weaves its tentacles around all of us so that no choice we seem to make is a pure or good choice. Not only is the individual sinful; the whole system of our living is sinful, and this is the Christian's tragic sense of life.

Those of us who have tried to be Christian in war know what this means. Perhaps some of you saw the movie or read the book *The Cruel Sea*. It's about a British destroyer assigned to escort and protect a convoy of ships going from England to Gibraltar in a sea teeming with enemy subs. The task is hopeless in many ways. The climax comes the last day out. The enemy has hit two ships in the squadron; they are sinking, and the survivors are floating around to be picked up. Suddenly the captain's sounding device registers on a submarine below. He follows the sound. He makes ready his depth charges. He moves his destroyer full steam ahead on the track. He knows he's coming to the spot where the enemy lies hidden below. Then he discovers that at that very spot are twenty survivors of one of his own British ships. He makes his decision, in a split second. He drops his depth charges, he kills them all, he hopes he's sunk the enemy submarine, he never knows. And every man on that ship, every British man of them, stands stock still, watching the captain. Watching for what? One thing—a gesture or word which will indicate whether the captain did what he had to do lightly and with an easy conscience.

It's not enough to say, "I did the best I could." There are times when the profound tragedy of many of our choices comes home to us. "Nothing you do is good; there's terrible evil against humanity in whatever you do, and you can't escape." This is the deeper meaning of sin which the Christian never avoids, the total predicament of sin. Sin is not only what one man ever does wrong; there's a sinful world around us of which we are very much a part, in which we may be lost.

This is the one thing that we can't escape as we look at the Cross of Jesus. What strikes us is that there is no one person who can be blamed for it. Legally Pilate can be blamed; he was the governor. But he was just carrying out Roman policy and doing it efficiently. Or the high priest can be blamed. But he had a religious institution at stake, and when he said, "It is better that one man die than that the people die," this makes sense, you can't blame him. So the mob can be blamed, or the disciples, or the Pharisees, but again this is no open-and-shut case. You see, the tragedy of the Cross, like the tragedy of the Cruel Sea, is not what one man as such ever did wrong; it's the total human situation, the endless predicament of our self-will, our goodness that takes the place of faith, our self-worship, our idolatry that takes the place of God. This is sin at its profoundest and most tragic level, the "body of this death," the world of sin. And in that world, says Jesus, you too may be lost like a coin, which the carelessness and evil of others have tossed under the carpet.

Some of us are *lost like the prodigal son*. What was his sin? That he went and had a good time in riotous living? Not particularly: that's for Hollywood. His sin was not in his immoralities but in his disloyalty to the father who loved him. It was not in his crimes but in his treason. That's an important distinction: crime is the breaking of law, but at least most criminals believe in law of some kind, and there's hardly a criminal that wants to do away with law itself. But treason is disloyalty to law itself, and as such is a far blacker evil than crime. Christianity has always thought of sin not so much in terms of the immoral act as in terms of the disloyalty involved. The prodigal was lost, not because he was immoral, but because he was disloyal.

Others of us, says Jesus, are *lost like the elder brother* in the story of the prodigal son. You may have forgotten him. He never left home. He thought he was good; he was self-satisfied and self-sufficient, he was virtuous. He never even felt lost in life. And here's where a lot of us belong at times. Ours is the sin of the elder brother, the sin of self-satisfaction and self-righteousness. Remember, according to Christianity, your virtues can keep you from God as much as your vices. Harlots get into the Kingdom of Heaven before Pharisees. The broken stand a better chance than the peddlers of pious platitudes. The wretched find God long before the respectable. Don't take my word for it: read your New Testament. The worst symptom of sin is always self-satisfaction. The only man never found by God is the man who never admits he's been lost, the elder brother.

This is the realism of the Christian faith. It never runs from the evil in the world; it's honest about sin. There's a dark side to human nature; there's a sad line to every human face. The Christian faith says quite simply that within him every man has a sense of having lost God and that every theory of human nature is shallow until it takes this into account. Man is an inveterate idolater; he places himself and his work rather than God at the center of creation—this is the essence of sin. The Christian faith goes on to say that this disease, this sense of being lost, has different symptoms. You may be lost like a sheep, bored and aimless. You may be lost like a coin, the victim of sinful circumstances. You may be disloyal like the prodigal son. And you may be self-satisfied like the elder brother, never admitting that you are lost, and thereby be more lost than ever. This is the sublime, the blunt honesty of Christianity. Nothing ever shocks a Christian once he's looked deep into his own heart. He has said, like the publican in the Scripture: "God be merciful to me a sinner."

One final word. I do not mean that human nature is depraved or life completely evil. Man may be a sinner; he is not a scoundrel. The image of the divine in all of us may be quite broken; it is never destroyed. On one side, the Christian is no shallow optimist. There's power to negative thinking in life as well as positive thinking if it's the power of truth. If you want to be a Christian you're going to have to think in depth, and live in depth, much deeper than you've ever done before. You will see the real tragedy of much that men call evil in life and the phoniness of much that men call good. The Christian is no shallow optimist about human nature.

But, on the other side, he's no shallow pessimist, either. According to the Christian faith, no man is ever completely lost to God. There's a pathetic longing for the good, there's a reaching out for the Eternal in every one of us, and often where you least expect it. Three years ago there was a riot of hardened criminals in the State Prison of Massachusetts. The authorities couldn't figure out what caused it. "Not the food," they said, "not the discipline; no, something stranger and more moving." Ted Green, one of the prisoners, tried to explain it to the newspapermen. "I've done a lot of bad things in my life, boys, a lot of evil things. My only wish now is that sometime I might do a good thing, like giving my eyes so a blind child might see. The trouble with life imprisonment is: you get to wondering, isn't there some way that I could do one good thing before I die, just one good thing?"

That's the amazing other side of human nature, the eternal longing in the darkest heart to do "one good thing before I die." The Christian believes in the goodness of man but only because he's been willing to understand his sinfulness. So, the first religious question you must ask is: "How real do I want to be, how honest?" If you'll never face the scandal of your life, you'll never see its glory. Christianity promises no half-way. It offers you no tranquilizer.

THREE

On Salvation

MANY of us have a negative reaction to the word "salvation," and it's probably healthy that we do. Salvation means a type of emotional, revival religion. It means the sawdust trail. We think of people who speak of being saved and are always self-righteous about it, always trying to get us saved just the way they are. We think of tent meetings, perhaps the Salvation Army and its lassies and brass band. Some of us think of the good-natured humor in the show *Guys and Dolls,* with all the gamblers getting converted at the mission. Salvation is the sawdust trail. We say quite honestly, "That's not for me."

Of course, the word "salvation" should have a wider meaning than that. As the early Christians used it the word meant simply deliverance, or rescue. Christianity for them was not essentially a philosophy of life; it was an experience of being lost and found, of being saved. And in essence, this is what Christianity has always been. There are religions of reform, and there are religions of rescue. In the main, Christianity has always been a religion of rescue, not necessarily the sawdust-trail type of rescue, but of rescue, nevertheless. Jesus may not save you in any one way, but he saves you: this is what every Christian understands.

Now I know what some of you are thinking: "Saves me from

what? Rescues me how? I've never been lost. As a matter of fact, I don't think I'm a sinner, anyway. I've had some bad conditioning here and there, but I'm working it out. I think these people who talk about salvation are really unhealthy and neurotic. Mine is a religion of self-improvement, social improvement. Let's make this world a better place in which to live and let's roll up our sleeves and get to work. Jesus was the first great welfare worker, wasn't he? He went about doing good. All I have to do is aim at his ideals. No one needs to rescue me or save me."

This comment is good so far as it goes; it depicts a religion of reform. Every age needs its reformers and ours not least of all. And a good deal that the churches talk about as salvation *is* unhealthy, and neurotic, and as thinking Christians we wouldn't want it. But is that the whole story? Isn't the Christ of the sociology seminar just as extreme as the Christ of the sawdust trail? Jesus went about doing good, but he also came "to seek and to save that which was lost" (Luke 19:10). No matter how you figure it, there must be some sense in which a great religion like Christianity rescues a person as well as reforms a person. There must be some way in which we all need to be saved.

Let me try to spell it out. First of all, the Christian faith says that, if we look at our lives in their deepest dimension and look at the world about us, we realize that in many ways we are quite helpless by ourselves; we are lost. This is why the religion of reform often doesn't reform. This is why methods of self-help often don't help: They're beside the point. It's as if, seeing a drowning man, instead of tossing him a life belt we toss him a book on *How to Be a Good Swimmer.* Reform religion doesn't always answer the real problem of the person.

The Christian faith says to each of us: deep in your life there are two experiences you must reckon with. *The first is the experience of moral paralysis,* the experience of knowing what's right and good and noble and not being able to do it or even choose it. The problem with most of us is not that of knowing what's good—we know; at least we know enough to better ourselves here and there. But something drags us back. We are not able to act on what we know, we haven't the power. Paul said:

"For the good that I would I do not: but the evil which I would not, that I do" (Rom. 7:19). And just to tell us to buck up and reform only increases the problem, makes us worse, sinks us deeper into our moral despair. My friends, you simply don't understand the twentieth century until you understand something of its terrible moral paralysis. Christopher Fry, the English poet, puts it: "We would rather be ruined than changed." And that speaks not only for our century; it speaks for each of us. Every one of us has had the terrifying experience of knowing the good and not being able to do the good.

Tied with this sense of moral paralysis is *the experience of estrangement from God, of utter aloneness in the universe,* an experience we've all had at times. This is what Colin Wilson describes in *The Outsider.* His outsider is not a sociological outsider, the man who didn't make the in-group. It is the man who has no cosmic home, has no frame of reference in the universe, is always a stranger to himself and his fellows, because he's a stranger to his Creator. This is what has been called "the riddle of the unhinged soul in the 20th century." This is what Thomas Wolfe so vividly describes: "Naked and alone we came into exile. In her dark womb we did not know our mother's face. From the prison of her flesh have we come into the unspeakable and uncommunicable prison of this earth. Who of us has known his brother? Which of us has looked into his father's heart? Which of us has not remained forever prison pent? Which of us is not forever a stranger and alone?" This is a beautiful passage to describe twentieth-century man, estranged from his fellows and his God, never at home in his universe, very much a stranger and alone.

Insofar as you have deeply felt these things, insofar as you have known something of the moral paralysis and the riddle of the unhinged soul of your century—and some of you have known it and felt it—a religion of rescue starts to make sense and Christianity can come to you as salvation. Man is not evil but man is in many ways strangely helpless. There is a certain sense in which every one of us is lost.

Christianity as salvation is, then, the experience of being helpless or lost and then the experience of being found. What do we mean by that? Well, if you've rightly understood your lostness, Christianity comes to you as great good news. It tells you something that changes your whole perspective and gives you a new power for living. It says that God's love has been made incarnate, has been made flesh in Jesus Christ, and that, if you once understand and believe in that love, you'll be found and not lost, you'll be rescued and saved.

To be more specific, what is the Christian perspective that changes your life? Christianity says, for one thing, that *God in his love finds you before you ever find him.* This is important. A religion of rescue always believes in the initiative of God more than the initiative of man. God reaches out in his love to you before you ever reach out toward him. This is real Good News to a man who is lost, to know that a rescue party has already started looking for him. This is the message of the Bible: "While we were yet sinners" (Rom. 5:8) (in other words, lost), God sent his only Son. God's love takes the initiative.

Not that we never seek for God; of course we do. But the Christian is always more amazed at God's search for him. The rescue party does most of the traveling, not the man who is lost. Long ago Job asked: "Canst thou by searching find out God?" (Job 11:7). And offhand the answer we give is: "Of course we can; let's get out the maps; let's start on a quest of the Eternal; let's be seekers in the things of the spirit." Good, that makes sense. But have you ever listened to the answers these "seekers" in the things of the spirit come back with? Most of them, at first, are quite disappointing: "God is the great beyond, God is the mysterious void, God is nothing, God is utter zero, God is that point at which parallel lines finally join in infinity, God is that force we can't describe that holds the molecules of the universe together, a kind of invisible paste." All of which, if we're honest with ourselves, are really quite disappointing answers. They're good to know, we say, and to seek for God is inescapable in our human make-up. But what *is* the good news that every seeker, every mystic, finally comes back with? Simply: God's seeking me. As Elton Trueblood puts it: "True religion is not man's search for the good life, important as that may be; neither is it our effort to find God, inevitable as that may be; true religion is our response to him who seeks us. It's not an argument for God, it's a response to God's love." I like that: it doesn't undercut religious aspiration. It *is* important to seek for the good life, and it *is* inevitable that we search for God, putting out our thousand feelers, turning our thousand spotlights into the great blackness of the heavens above us. But that's not the essence of Christianity. Christianity is a response to the God who seeks us. It's Good News, the good news that you haven't found God but God has found you.

Secondly, a religion of rescue not only talks about the initiative of God's love, *it talks about how God's love suffers in your behalf.* Here we come into the inner mysteries of Christianity. We worship a Cross. Why? Simply because it's beautiful? No. Simply because it reminds us of an event in history, Good Friday, April 7, A.D. 30, when a carpenter hung long hours on a Roman Cross? No. We worship a Cross because it reminds us of the Christian faith that interpreted that event by saying: "Christ died for our sins."

Or we have Holy Communion. We take the bread and the wine along with the sacred words of Jesus: "This is my body, broken for you. . . ." You say: "What does that mean?" Well, I can't tell you everything it means, but let me just say this. When you commit a sin who pays for it? Offhand you say, "I do." But really, do you? Is the account balanced up that neatly in this universe? No, actually your parents may suffer for your sin as much as you ever do, and your children who come after you, and certainly your friends. In other words, we are all the benefactors of the suffering love of others, all of us. In the strange justice of the universe love often takes our place, stands between us and the judgment we deserve. So, Christians have said that this is true of God, as seen in the Cross of Jesus Christ. He is the Lamb of God that taketh away the sin of the world; he stands as if he were in our place.

During World War II there was a wonderful Russian nun, Mother Maria. She lived in Paris under the Nazis and did her best to relieve the suffering not only of the Catholics but of the Jews under persecution. But one day, when the Nazis were lining up the Jewish girls in her convent-school to take them off to the execution chambers, one high-school girl was so frightened that

Mother Maria took off her nun's habit, quickly put over her head the yellow scarf of the Jew and said gently: "I'll go for you; I'll take your place." And Mother Maria died as a Jew. You see, there is such a thing in this world as suffering in behalf of others. Christianity says that God suffers that way too. This is the meaning of the Cross. Christ went in our place.

The third feature of a religion of rescue is that it talks about how *God's love accepts you as you are.* This is what the Christian means when he says that God's love is "gracious." The Christian knows that he never merits the love of God. You'll never be that good, you'll never measure up. The Christian is one who never lives under the tyranny of perfection, what Karen Horney, the psychologist, rightly calls "the tyranny of the should." "I should do this, I should be this, I should be perfect as God wants me to be." Moral and religious bookkeeping is as much out of place before the love of God as counting the notes would be while listening to a Mozart symphony. No, the Christian is the man who simply accepts God's love; it's a gift, not something you merit or work to secure. Acceptance is the basis of the Christian life, not striving after moral perfection.

This is what Christianity as a religion of rescue always says about God. You can think of him as the perfectionist father, and then you'll try to merit his favor, working your moral muscles: so many good deeds, so many alms given, so many laws kept, so much bookkeeping. But that's a dead end. You'll end up under the "tyranny of the should." But if you live by faith, accept the fact that you are accepted, come home, even as you are, then a new peace and radiance and freedom comes into your life. This is salvation, this is Christianity as rescue. This is being found.

When Holy Week comes each year, you can pass it by without so much as one thought. It can be just another week, or it can be a week that will change your life. You can find real Christianity—not Christianity as a philosophy of life to help you get along, important as that may be, nor as an ethical code of some sort, important again as that may be, but Christianity as salvation, deliverance, rescue, a totally new way of looking at things. You'll have to start with yourself and your world. You'll have to look below the surface. In many ways, in spite of your assured exterior, you are quite helpless and lost, and you know it. You're grown up enough to know that we all suffer from a sense of moral paralysis —knowing what's good but so often not having the power to do it. And we suffer often enough from a sense of estrangement from God, what the poet has called "the distance of God." Perhaps you'll turn to your Bible and just read the life of Jesus, honestly, prayerfully. There you will find what Christianity is saying, what makes it still the best Good News to mankind. You think you're seeking for God, but God is even more seeking for you: that's Good News. God's love suffers for your sins; even Deity is not immune: that's Good News. God's love accepts you as you are: that's Good News. Let these truths sink into your heart and you'll be quite a different person. You'll never be shocked by another person's sin, because you'll know how lost and sinful you can be. You'll never be a moralist, because you'll know that virtue never merits love, much less God's love. You'll never be a perfectionist, because a perfectionist always plays God. You'll live in a new dimension, a dimension of gratitude and of humility. A rescued man is always different; he can't help but be. He changes, he's reformed, but he's reformed because he's been rescued. This is deliverance. This is new life to the soul.

One of the most bitter enemies of the early Christians said of them: "These Christians are always happy, always in the full bloom of thought, always at springtime." He simply couldn't understand it, the joy of salvation: "Jesus not only reforms me, he rescues me!" To believe this is to keep life always at springtime.

FOUR

On the Trinity

WHAT is the Christian understanding of God? I'm going to be so bold as to say that the Christian understanding of God is the understanding of God as the Blessed Trinity. I know that sounds pious, I know it sounds remote to many of you, I know that those of you who have studied Western civilization will remember the endless and somewhat silly arguments of the various Church councils of the third through the fifth centuries. For instance, "The Catholic faith is this, that we worship one God in Trinity and Trinity in unity, neither confounding the persons nor dividing the substance; and in this trinity none is afore or after other, none is greater or less than another, but the whole three persons are coeternal together and coequal." That's a mouthful, to say the least—what someone has called "the arithmetic of bloodless categories." No wonder we give up, no wonder we honestly say: "I believe in God, but not all that stuff."

Well, let me say right off that as a definition of God I'm not sure the Trinity does make sense. Can we define God anyway, adequately define him? The French have a proverb: *"Dieu defini est Dieu finis."* It means a God defined is a God finished. That's probably right. There is no definition adequate for God. He is a mystery and we had better not forget that. In the Scripture (Exod.

33:18–20) Moses says to God, "Show me thy glory." To which God replies: "No man shall see my face and live." But according to the story, God hid Moses in the cleft of the rock and, while he could not see his face, Moses could see God's back as he went by. In other words, God can be real to man but he can never be plainly or fully seen. Yes, God defined, even as Trinity, is to some extent a God finished.

But if the Trinity does not define God it certainly shows us a way to worship God. And that's what the doctrine of the Trinity as held in the Christian Church really is: it's a worship symbol. The Creed I quoted before says: "We *worship* God as Trinity." The word "Trinity" abounds largely in our worship services. There's the hymn, "Holy, holy, holy . . . God in three persons blessed trinity." There's the benediction: "The grace of our Lord Jesus Christ, the love of God, the communion of the Holy Spirit be with you now and evermore." At the baptism of children or as you stand before the marriage altar the minister will bless you "in the name of the Father, Son and Holy Ghost." Much of our choir music is devoted to praise of the Trinity. The Trinity is a way Christians worship God, even if he cannot be defined.

What is the doctrine of the Trinity? Essentially this: the Christian faith says that when we worship God we must be careful to worship him in his fullness. Often you and I can settle down with a very small understanding of God: God is the great power behind nature, or the biological *élan vital,* or an abstraction—where two lines meet in infinity. Or maybe God for us is Jesus: we even pray to Jesus, "Dear Jesus, take care of me." Or maybe God is just human love, or the divine in man. All of these may tell us something about God: they may be right, but for the Christian they are partial. If you want to worship God fully, you worship him as Father, Son, and Spirit, three persons in one, the Trinity.

Or since the word "persons" implies separate individuals for most of us, which it never meant to the early Church, then let's put it: you must always see God revealing himself in three activities, equally important and continuous. You must worship God as father, the Creator, the one who not only created the earth but is even now creating all things. You must worship God as the Son, revealing himself in history, particularly in the life and death of Jesus the Christ—God is always concrete and active in history. And God the Spirit—that, too, cannot be forgotten—the God who touches each human life and speaks today to each of us in the fellowship of the Church. That's what the Christian understands by God. God is a mystery: we never see his face. But what we do see of him, we know we must worship in his fullness. And to be seen fully he must be seen as three activities, as Trinity.

Let me break this concept down and try to suggest what it can mean for each of us personally. First of all, let me suggest this: *the Trinity says that God by his very nature must be outgoing.* He must express himself, he must be eternally creative. God the Father cannot be alone; he must express himself through the Son and the Spirit. Phillips Brooks used to say of the Trinity that it was "the great social concept of God." You see, people who don't believe in the Trinity usually speak of God as a lonely aristocrat. He may be the God of the philosophers, sitting solitary and spinning out his thoughts. He may be the God of the deists, the genius who invented this universe and set it together like a perfectly ticking watch and then left it—God the inventor-genius—still essentially solitary, alone. But in the Trinity the Christian faith totally rejects this idea. The essence of God's nature is to be constantly expressing himself, to be outgoing. As Professor Palmer of Harvard once wrote of his wife, Alice Freeman: "Built for bounty, she held nothing back." The Trinity says the God we worship is like that: built for bounty, he holds nothing back. That's his nature. The Trinity is the great social concept of God.

That's why I've always admired the Fathers of the Church who for 300 or more years hammered away at this doctrine of the Trinity. They asserted the greatness of God as much as did the Jews but they instinctively knew how greatness, even in God, can become lonely and self-centered. Recently I was reading the life of Enrico Caruso, the operatic tenor. If any man ever achieved a fabulous greatness in our century it was Caruso. The only musical education he ever had was to sit in the corner while the maestro gave another boy six voice lessons. He could sing basso as well as tenor. Caruso had genius all right, but with it what self-centeredness! He was in a hotel in San Francisco at the time of the terrible earthquake. With all humanity suffering around him he stayed up in his room practicing his vocal exercises. And what utter loneliness there was in his greatness, too! When he was on his deathbed not a single doctor in all Europe would operate; no one wanted to take the chance of killing Caruso. So, no doubt, in our world greatness often goes hand in hand with self-centeredness and loneliness. Up to the time of the Church Fathers this was essentially the philosophic concept of God himself, the solitary genius, the detached thinker, the aristocrat. And the early Christians instinctively said no to that concept. God himself cannot run the risk of self-centeredness. By nature he must always express himself, be outgoing, hold nothing back. God is one but he is not the lonely one.

Let's go on. The doctrine of the Trinity says not only that God by his very nature must always express himself but that *he has become most perfectly expressed, has become concrete in history, in the person of Jesus Christ.* Jesus, of course, was human: only a few early heresies have ever denied that. "Being wearied he sat thus on the well." "Jesus wept" as he stood before the grave. Like other men he asked questions: "Who touched me? How many loaves have ye?" He was tempted as we are, yet without sin. Facing the Cross, he knelt in the Garden and the anguish poured forth from his brow like great drops of blood falling to the ground. Yes, Jesus was bone of our bone and flesh of our flesh. But when it was all over, men looked back and said something more: "In the beginning was the Word, and the Word was with God, and the Word was God. . . . And the Word became flesh, and dwelt among us [literally: "pitched his tent among us"], (and we beheld his glory, the glory as of the only begotten of the Father,) full of grace and truth" (John 1:1, 14). And that's the second meaning of the doctrine of the Trinity. In this human life of a Galilean Carpenter the eternal God pitched his tent among men. In this great one deed in history he spoke most clearly and Jesus is his Word.

This, of course, is the Christian interpretation of history and it is quite frankly an interpretation. But all history is an interpretation of some sort, there is no such thing as a bald uninterpreted fact, much as we like to think so. And this interpretation of history is why the Gospel was so exciting 1900 years ago and is so exciting today. It was Good News. Why? Because those early Christians told the Greeks and Romans that another teacher had appeared on the horizon? Not at all: Socrates and Seneca were more than a match for a humble carpenter. Or that there was another prophet among the prophets? Essentially no. Perhaps then it was that Jesus had discovered God as no other man ever had, that he was "the greatest and best believer that ever lived." No, the apostles never preached that. The Good News was not that man had found God but that God had found man, that God had revealed himself in the dust and soil of our history. We're always talking about the responsiveness of man to the divine, but Christians are amazed at the initiative of God. As students we talk about the search for God. God is hiding somewhere and religion is a serious and lofty game of hide-and-seek. This is all right, so far as it goes, but it does not go far enough. For the Christian it's only halfway. The other half of religion is God's search for you. You're the one running away and hiding but God doesn't give up. He's what Francis Thompson called "The Hound of Heaven."

> I fled Him, down the nights and down the days;
> I fled Him, down the arches of the years;
> I fled Him, down the labyrinthine ways
> Of my own mind; and in the mist of tears
> I hid from Him, and under running laughter . . .
> > [sounds like the average student
> > But you can't escape from God, the
> > Hound of Heaven, from . . .]
> Those strong feet that followed, followed after.
> But with unhurrying chase,
> And unperturbèd pace,
> Deliberate speed, majestic instancy.[1]

And if it's this initiative of God that strikes your heart as you look over your life, then what could be more beautiful and meaningful than the thought that God took the initiative in history, in

[1] *Selected Poems of Francis Thompson* (New York: Dodd, Mead & Co., 1925).

the life of Jesus the Christ? At least, that's what Christians think and believe. That's what they mean by God the Son. You see, if the Trinity says that God cannot be lonely, it also says that God cannot be abstract; it's his nature to be active and concrete in time, not far off, removed, something at the long-distant end of some mathematical equation. Actually the only way we men know God is through an incarnation, a person, an event in history. I once had a Sunday School class. I asked the youngsters to draw a picture of a good boy, for what reason I don't know. Most of them drew abstractions, a boy with hair combed, shoes shined, suit pressed— a boy who obviously never existed. But one youngster drew another picture, a boy taking his little sister by the hand to cross the street in front of traffic. Not an abstraction but a concrete deed in time— that's what goodness is. And that, says the Christian, is what God is, God as seen in his second activity, the second person of the Trinity. God is never abstract; he's always active in history. He even sent his Son to dwell among us, to reveal the wondrous love of his Father-heart.

We cannot stop there; too often we do. When we Christians worship God, we not only worship him as Father-Creator, constantly outgoing and expressing himself and creating; we not only worship him as Son, concrete and active in history, particularly in the life of Jesus the Christ; we also worship God as the Holy Spirit, the third person or function of the mystery we call God. It's a wonderful thought. When you think of God the Holy Spirit, you are reminded that God can never be just in the past. So often we can think of God the Father creating the universe and letting it go at that. So often we can think of God the Son as the life of Jesus back there in Palestine 2000 years ago. But God the Spirit, dwelling in the hearts of believers and in the life of the Church, is very much among us today. And the wonderful thing about the doctrine of the Trinity is that it says that that work of God, the work of the Spirit in our hearts, is equal to the work of Creation or the work of Christ. The Trinity is no dead, theological dogma; it's really a way of life, a life of the Spirit with all the humility and hope that implies.

Holy Spirit dwell with me
I myself would holy be.

God himself is complete only in the lives of men and women who dare to be divinely possessed.

This is it, then. You ask me to define God? I cannot; no man has ever seen his face. You ask me how Christians understand God? They understand God in worship. You ask me how they worship? I'd say they worship God in Trinity. And to worship him as Trinity you worship him in all his fullness. As a reverent scientist you see God in his Creation, but that's only part of it— God the Father. As a reverent historian you see God the Son: if history is "the story of uniqueness," as it has often been defined, then Jesus the Christ is unique to the reverent historian. As a reverent psychologist you might worship God as the Holy Spirit, but again that's only part of it. God in the fullness of his glory is lord of history, lord of psychology, lord of science, partly under-stood by each and yet greater than all. When we would settle for less, the doctrine of the Trinity is a constant reminder and warning to us Christians: "Your God is not big enough."

FIVE

On the Church

THE second chapter of Acts describes the birthday of the Christian Church, the incident called Pentecost or sometimes Whitsunday. The disciples were gathered together in prayer, each with his memories of the Lord Jesus, how he lived, how he died upon the Cross, how he rose from the dead. Suddenly, the room seemed to be filled with a mighty wind, and individual tongues of flame sat on the head of each person present, and they knew that the Spirit of the Risen Christ was among them. This is symbolic and colorful language describing what the Church really is. Each Christian has his own inner experience of Christ, the tongue of fire on his head. But the Church is more than individual experiences of Christ; it's a group experience as well, a mighty wind that fills the whole house. This is the way the Spirit of Christ comes to us, on the one hand individually—religion is the most private part of a person, defined by Whitehead as "what a man does with his solitariness." But that's only half of it. Christ comes to the Christian as he worships in a group, as he shares the Christian life with others, as he joins in praise with others. There is no such thing as a solitary Christian. A person is a Christian within a community. That community is the Church.

Now I know it's hard at times for many of us, particularly in college, to appreciate the Church, or any specific local church we may know. As students we are not especially interested in institutions of any sort. We are just starting to enjoy our freedom as young adults, and institutions always cramp our freedom to some extent. They are big, they are slow, they are corrupt, they are often tyrannical, they put chains on every idealist. I stood recently in the Jefferson Memorial in Washington and read those great words of his around the rotunda: "I have sworn eternal warfare against any form of tyranny over the minds of men." Well, that's the way we feel about most institutions: they are tyrants, often in subtle ways, but tyrants none the less over our minds, our hearts, our ideals.

We feel this way most strongly about religion. We all say, "I have my own religion. I think it's rather profound in its own way. But when I look at institutionalized Christianity, when I get into the Church, frankly I get disillusioned." We go on: "I've learned enough history to know that the Church has been responsible for much misery and bloodshed in human life. I've learned enough sociology to know that the Church is often the most conservative social institution in the country. Isn't the most segregated institution in America today the Christian Church? I've learned enough economics to know that most churches are class churches and follow the economic thinking of the group they comprise: think of the Russian Orthodox church backing up with its wealth and jewels all the reactionary czars; think of that church in New York City whose tower, symbolically enough, was found a few years ago to be leaning nineteen inches toward Wall Street. I've learned enough education to know that the Sunday School is 'the most wasted hour in the week.' As to the ministers, well, they're 'politicians' just like the rest of us." Isn't that the way we talk, and isn't that the way we think, all of us, myself included, often enough? Individual Christianity is one thing, this institutionalized Christianity quite another. To keep the one you may have to steer pretty clear of the other.

Now this is a sizable and a healthy indictment. And let me say right off: I know of no profound or mature churchman who has not at one time or another been in revolt against the Church,

against Christianity as an institution. I might even go on and say
that every mature Christian is always in some revolt against the
Church, always at tension with it, every day of his life. In other
words, you'll never be a Christian churchman until you've learned
to see through the institution, to hate institutionalism, and particularly religious institutionalism, as such. Jefferson was right: there
are tyrannies against which we should swear eternal warfare, and
the Christian institution is not exempt.

Having said this, I would like to describe from my own experience, during and after college, how I learned to move over
from the stage of simple revolt to a growing appreciation of the
Church. I could make my point abstractly, but let me put it
personally. I think it may help you more in your own Christian
life. Individually, we may be sincere and growing Christians, but
what makes us churchmen?

First of all, *I found I had to learn more facts about the Church.*
The Church is a big institution, the most international and most
universal institution in the world today, over 600 millions strong.
I found that most of the so-called facts I had acquired about the
Church were partial at best. There was a lot to be said on the other
side—about the Church and segregation, or the Church and
economic classes, or the hypocrisy of the clergy, or the bloodshed
of the Church, or its persecutions, or that most wasted hour of the
week called the Sunday School. I found that, just factually speaking, I was the proverbial blind man who was judging the whole
elephant by the piece of its tail I happened to be holding. So my
advice to you is: balance up your facts on the Church.

Secondly, *I developed over a period of time a certain sense of
humor about the average church.* You see, as an idealist in college,
I was taking the Church too seriously and defining it wrongly. The
Church is a society of sinners who have known the grace of God,
not a society of saints. And nothing is funnier than a society of
sinners trying to be a society of saints. Toynbee once said: "Religion is the most serious business of mankind." But just because
religion is so serious, people engaged in religion can be completely comical. In church, people are always trying to be at their
best and that is why you need above all else a sense of humor in

church work. I recall one delightful old lady who always shook my hand at the close of the morning service and tried to say something good. But one day she slipped and said, "Pastor, every sermon you preach is better than the *next.*" The point is that in time you soften your attitude toward the Church when you realize that nothing is funnier than a group of human beings trying to act better than they really are. You become more of a churchman when you learn to love people and realize that we all have a certain awkwardness in the house of, or presence of, God.

Thirdly, *I discovered that groups don't necessarily level off individual idealism,* that, on the contrary, sometimes Christians in groups can be more idealistic than those same Christians as individuals. This may seem strange to you but it's often true. I know of a well-known minister who had a church in an area where segregation was very strict for any Negroes. This minister invited a classmate from seminary, a Negro, to preach for him and stay in his home overnight. Much of his membership, being southern in social convention, was affronted by this act. The deacons called a special meeting to have it out with the minister. To a man they agreed this was a wrong thing for their minister to do. But when the meeting was finally called to order, after an awkward prayer and equally awkward silence, the chairman spoke: "We all know why we're here, to tell our minister that in this town you can't have a Negro in your home. As an individual, I haven't changed my mind a bit on that, but you know, sitting here as a church, it looks different, and I don't even want to call for a vote." And the rest agreed. You see, as young people we usually think the individual Christian is good and the Church drags his idealism down. But the opposite may be the case, too: never forget it. As individuals we are often prejudiced and erring and weak, and it's the fellowship, the mystic ties of Christians bound together in the love of God, that lifts us up and saves us from ourselves. You may have to live a while to realize that sometimes the Church is something greater and nobler and more than the sum of the individuals who compose it. The group has a spiritual life of its own.

The fourth thing I learned is that *you never grow in religion by soliloquy;* you grow by conversation. I found that I needed the

Christian group around me in order to keep and define my own individual faith. Modern life is solitary enough. We are "a society of onlookers, congested but lonely." And so the only way a Christian grows is by relationship. You can never be a Robinson Crusoe in matters of religious faith, living on your intellectual island. You wither and die if you don't share your faith.

So much, then, for the value of the Church, at least as one Christian has found it. Now let me put this in more positive terms. What is the Christian understanding of the Church? What is it like to someone on the inside? How can we express not only the human side of the Church but its divine mission?

Here, I suppose, each Christian becomes a bit of a poet. He uses similes and pictures to express what the Church means to him and his fellow believers. The New Testament uses certain pictures. The Church is an *ecclesia* (Matt. 16:18), meaning an assembly called for a special purpose, as the ancient Greeks were called out to the gate of the city to discuss civic affairs. Or the Church is the Body of Christ (Eph. 1:22–23), organic rather than organizational. Christ is the head of the body and each of us has a necessary function within the Church, no matter how lowly. Or the Church is a *koinonia,* a fellowship of believers (Gal. 2:9). Or the Church is an ark (I Pet. 3:20), like the ark of Noah rescuing men from drowning. Or the Church is called, by Paul, a colony of heaven (Phil. 3:20—Moffatt translation): churchmen are really citizens of two worlds, like early colonists, apart from and yet still part of the old country from which they came. These are pictures, every one of them, New Testament pictures of the Church, and meaningful over many years to Christians.

But perhaps as modern Christians we might try to capture the same meanings in different pictures. Some come to my mind. *I think of the Church as a giant library.* Now a library can be looked upon as a dead place, a mausoleum of some sort, where various authors have their graves marked by books. But a library is a living thing, really; it is memory, it is thought communicated from the past and becoming part of you and me. It's an incarnation of others into your life; it's an extension of personality from the past. It's the lengthened shadow of the great.

So the Church is a living memory of Jesus Christ. It's an extension of the Incarnation into modern life. It's the Body of the Risen Christ, living now, the past made present, as in a library. Every church is a fellowship that remembers Jesus Christ and more than remembers—actively participates in his spirit, whether by creeds, or by rituals, or by the Holy Communion or the Mass. If every institution is the lengthened shadow of a great personality through time, then the Church is the lengthened shadow of Jesus the Christ through all the changes of history.

And the Church is like a hospital: that's another modern picture that comes to mind. It helps people, it cures men's souls, it meets human needs. The Bible calls the Church an Ark in this regard, but I'm afraid an Ark means little to most of us. A hospital, however, means a great deal when you're sick or dying. And in modern life the Christian Church must always meet the desperate needs of people as a good hospital does.

The problem is: what do people need, what's their disease? Here, like a good doctor, or a good hospital, you have to distinguish the symptom from the disease. Churches are always tempted to treat symptoms. We people are lonely, we are "the lonely crowd," so churches offer fellowship to the lonely. But it must be fellowship on a deeper level than that of the Lonely Hearts Club or the local fraternities. Loneliness is the symptom and not the disease, and if your church is just friendly and nothing more, you'll make people all the lonelier, lonely in a big crowd; this loneliness is the worst. People need a morale boost, a lift. So the church is tempted to be a pep rally, a vitamin dispenser of some sort, a mental gymnasium where you can practice exercises that make you feel better and better every day. A lot of modern preaching has been called "psychology with organ music." But when all is said and done, there is a desperate need for spiritual help these days, and that's the Church's job, to meet people at the level of their deepest and most desperate need, that of God. As Charles Malik of the United Nations has put it, "Every tragedy in history has arisen because somewhere, somehow, man has misinterpreted himself. He took himself to be what he was not, or not to be what he was. You and I are not only political animals. Nor certainly are we mere creatures of desire and lust, wanting today a shack, tomorrow a palace, today a bicycle, tomorrow an airplane. No, you and I will walk barefooted and sleep on the floor if only our deeper moral and spiritual needs are recognized and met."[1] That's the midnight cry from the heart of twentieth-century man. The Church is a hospital to answer that cry.

So every church is like a library—you might call this "the mystic church" of her Lord. And every church is like a good hospital—this is "the subjective church," "the church that meets my needs." But finally, *every church is like an art museum.* What do I mean? An art museum not only takes care of people's needs; it also has to be true to art, to glorify art, quite apart from people's immediate needs. A good art museum gives people what they want, or what they think they need in art, but that's only part of its function. A good art museum has a higher duty, which is to be true to beauty, to culture, to the best in art. It is the same for the Christian Church. The Church is here, not only to take care of people's needs, but to be true to the Gospel, to the Faith. On the one hand, it has a duty to people, like a hospital. On the other, it has a duty to glorify God, quite apart from the sickness of the age of which it is a part. This is the Church at worship. This is the objective Church. This is the Church age after age lifting holy hands to God in prayer. This is the eternal Church. This is the Church against which, as our Lord promised, the gates of hell shall never prevail.

My wife, my son, and I go to Maine every summer. We return to Granville on the road from the north. This road is over hill and dale. For the last fifteen miles of our trip we play a game in the car. Each of us guesses when we will see the spire of the Chapel of the University as we ride over each hill. And when the first one sees it, he always shouts, "There it is, there it is!"

I believe the Christian always has some such sense of the Church: "Whether I like it or not, whether it satisfies me or not, there it is—to the glory of God!"

[1] Charles Malik, Commencement Address, Denison University, Granville, Ohio, June, 1952.

Eternal as the eternal hills
Immovable she stands
A mountain that shall fill the earth
A house not made with hands.

SIX

On Hell

EVERY so often a student challenges me: "What about hell? You don't believe in silly notions like that, do you?" He usually goes on to explain how much he has outgrown the religion with which he came to college, how he can't see the point of much theology, especially the various articles of the Apostles' Creed he once repeated in church with so much gusto. One of the first articles to go is "he descended into hell." What modern person can believe in hell?

As a starter, I'm sure we could all agree with the student, that there are a lot of silly ideas about hell we should get rid of, gross misconceptions. I dare say the average one of us thinks of hell as a place, with flames, and devils and pitchforks. This we must understand is not the picture the Bible gives. It comes from two sources, the paintings of the Middle Ages and the writings of John Milton, particularly in *Paradise Lost*. Medieval theology made God a terrible judge. In Michelangelo's "Last Judgment" you see God on a high throne, separating the souls of men, sending some to bliss and others to eternal torment. You can actually feel them tumbling into huge tongues of fire. That's the medieval picture. God was a judge and he sentenced men to hell. Then came Milton, and most of us can still remember the descriptions in *Paradise Lost*

—Satan and Beelzebub and Lucifer carrying pitchforks and walking around with tails. Great poetry this is, yes, but remember it's poetry. Don't try to convert its symbols into fact; don't say that's what God is like or that's the geography of the future life. It's not at all, for Christians. Christians must get rid of such ideas of hell.

Actually, the Bible has two words for hell, and they both are picture words. The first is the Hebrew word "Sheol," which is like the Greek "Hades." It means the place of departed spirits. It has no thought that you are wicked. It's just where you go when you die. This is what the Apostles' Creed means when it says that "Jesus descended into hell." It doesn't mean he was a bad or wicked man. It simply means he tasted death to the full; he truly died on the Cross; he was numbered with the departed; he went to Sheol. This is the first biblical meaning of hell: the place of all departed spirits.

The second word is more interesting. It's the word you find in the New Testament. It's the word Jesus used in the Scripture: "If thy hand offend thee, cut it off; it is better for thee to enter into life maimed, than having two hands to go into hell" (Mark 9:43). And he goes on to add: "Where their worm dieth not, and the fire is not quenched." The word Jesus uses is the word "Gehenna." It's the name of a place, the valley of Hinnom just outside the walls of Jerusalem. This valley had a very bad name among Jews. It was the place where foreign gods had been worshiped and human sacrifice carried on. The Jews thought there was a curse on the valley; they still do. A friend was over there a couple of years ago and he said that someone had built apartments on the edge of the valley of Hinnom, but everyone moved out when they heard it was hell; no one dared to live there. And because this valley was cursed it was used as a city dump. Everything that was useless was thrown there; the fires were kept burning night and day. So you get Jesus' picture. Approaching the Holy City of Jerusalem he couldn't overlook right before his eyes the valley of Hinnom. And so he speaks of hell, Gehenna, the valley of Hinnom, "where their worm dieth not, and the fire is not quenched."

Keeping this terrible picture in mind—and remember it is only a picture—what do Christians mean by hell? First of all, this picture should remind us that *hell is where life is wasted*. The city dump is filled with waste, things that were once good and useful now are largely no good and useless. So are many human lives, says Jesus. "Of all sad words of tongue and pen, the saddest are these—it might have been." Josiah Royce, the Harvard philosopher, used to speak of "the hell of the irrevocable"—the things you can't call back, the things you might have been but never will be. That's the first inkling we human beings have of the meaning of hell: it's where life is wasted.

Some of us, who have lived through a great war, perhaps two, know the meaning of this. The terrible thing about war is not the material destruction; cities will rise again on the dust of other cities. But you can't call back the men, the life, the million young men with their dreams, their hopes, their spiritual insights, their plans for a better world. That's the hell of it, a whole generation eaten away, wasted, lost. I can still see Bishop Fjellbu of Norway, holding up those hands that had known the shackles of Hitler's prisons and saying pathetically: "At the end of the first world war, Europe was full of prophets. Many of them were false prophets with false messages. But today we have no prophets in Europe and the young men have no message." That is the horror of war—not the waste of property but the waste of soul. There are no prophets left. You can't call them back to life.

And what can be said of a generation can certainly be said of us as individuals. The most you can say about some people is: "What a waste." If only you could call them back to what they might have been, but some things can't be called back, and let's not fool ourselves. You remember a few summers ago there was a young fellow, named Ted Sierks, who fell overboard in the Hawaiian yacht races. For thirty hours he floated alone in shark-infested waters. When he was rescued, the reporters say he had a strange look on his face, as if he had been in another world. And when they asked him what he thought about all that time floating so near sudden death, his answer was: "I thought about the time, all the time I had wasted in my life." I think that's a strange and terrible thought, enough to change the face of any one of us.

Sometimes I honestly wonder as I look at some of my students whether someday they may not wake up and look back on their four years at college—four years when vast horizons of the mind and the spirit could be opened to them—and say, "Oh, what a waste of good time." But then it won't do them any good: that's the brutal fact of life. We can't call back days that have gone. That's hell, everybody's hell, where life is wasted. It's the terrible valley of Hinnom, where the worm dieth not and the fire, the inner fire of the heart, is never quenched.

But let's go on. Hell is not only where life is wasted; *hell is where life has no meaningful relationships to others.* This, too, Jesus must have had in mind as he looked over that city dump outside Jerusalem. Here was a whole valley filled with things that people no longer had any use for. So far as the human family was concerned, they were lost, they had no value, no one cared. And carrying that picture out, hell is that state, both in this life and in the life-to-come, of utter self-centeredness. You don't belong to anyone, no one belongs to you. Hell is where life has no meaningful relationships to others. It's really the place where there is no love.

In this sense, of course, we all know that there is plenty of hell on earth, perhaps right here. Talk to any psychiatrist, visit any mental hospital, and you'll see what I mean; person after person is so ingrown, so completely concerned with self that he can't establish relationships with anybody or any reality beyond himself. He is, as it were, on the trash heap of life, and the torments he endures John Milton himself could not describe. And lest we feel self-righteous, to a certain degree let's admit we are all tempted to such self-centeredness, such stultifying egocentricity. Sarah Bernhardt, the world's greatest actress at the turn of the century, admitted she played the part of Ophelia a hundred times before she ever knew how *Hamlet* ended. Her interest always died in the play, she says, "when she went off the stage." Well, that's a picture of many people you and I know, of ourselves often enough, self-centered, ingrown, not interested when our little ego is off the stage. And that's where hell begins in each of us, where we're alone, all alone on the stage with ourselves.

The New Testament has a word for this state of the soul. It's the terrible word "lost." "The Son of man is come to seek and to save that which was lost" (Luke 19:10), we are told. But what does it mean to be lost? It means simply to be without any meaningful relationships, that's all. I'm not lost in New York City because 92 Fifth Avenue, where I'm standing, has a relationship to 96 Fifth Avenue, which in turn has a relationship with 34th Street and the Long Island Railroad and the town of Flushing where I lived for a dozen years, all a series of meaningful relationships. But take me out to Iowa and put me in one of those cornfields and I'd be lost; unfortunately cornstalks don't have numbers, and without numbers I have no geography, no meaningful relation to the world about me. And that's what the New Testament means by lost; a man or woman is lost who is so completely self-centered that all meaningful relationships with other people, with noble causes, with God himself have been severed, leaving nothing but the lonely ego constantly to look at itself in the mirror. That's the meaning of hell, according to Jesus. It's where life has no value, no meaningful relationships to others. It's that dreary valley filled with things nobody cares about.

All of which brings me to the most difficult and most terrible thought of all; hell is not only where life is wasted and where life has no meaningful relationship to others, but *it's that state of a person's soul where even God cannot seem to help.* Our fathers used to say that hell was separation from God. The valley of Hinnom, according to the Jews, was the one place on earth that couldn't seem to be redeemed from its idolatry, that God himself couldn't hallow. So Jesus, looking at that great refuse heap just outside the walls of the Holy City, must have had the same terrifying thought. In the geography of the soul there is a place where the worm dieth not and the fire is not quenched, a point where even the love of God cannot seem to save.

Now let's get this straight. Hell is not the doctrine that God abandons men; it's the doctrine that men abandon God. It's not the doctrine that God ceases to love the sinner; in the light of the revelation of Jesus Christ we can never believe that. But it is the doctrine, the grand doctrine, if you please, of the freedom of man, the eternal freedom of man. God will never force anyone to believe in him, or to obey him, or to love him; the latch is still on the inside of the door through all eternity. The Father will knock and knock, but he will never break that door down. Man, you are free, forever free: that's what the doctrine of hell reminds us. And if freedom means anything, it means the freedom to throw yourself away, the freedom, if you so choose, to be forever lost.

For this reason, then, I believe that hell has a very practical importance in our Christian lives. Most of us treat life entirely too lightly, I'm afraid. We say, "What difference does it make what I do or choose or think?" But hell reminds us it does make a difference. Life is in earnest, and if our freedom is eternal, then every day we choose between life and death. Every hour we look toward God or toward destruction. We stand between heaven and hell. This is why Jesus had such an earnestness in his message, such an offensive earnestness, as he looked at Gehenna. "If thy hand offend thee, cut it off; if thy foot offend thee, cut it off; if thine eye offend thee, pluck it out." Did he mean we were to multilate our bodies? Not at all. But he did mean that what your hand may choose, what your foot may do, what your eye may see can take you moment by moment on the road either to heaven or to hell. That's how important our decisions are in this life; they determine character, and character stands for all eternity. It's the splendor and the terror of being free.

So, if this picture of hell does nothing else it ought constantly to remind us to choose and live wisely. Many scholars believe that it was Père Groot who wrote *The Imitation of Christ.* As a young man he was watching a game, when someone in the stands, we don't know who, tapped him sharply on the shoulder. "Friend," he said, "thou shouldst be a different man."

Well, Christians, that's the ultimate meaning of hell. It's a sharp tap on the shoulder when we're inclined to laugh life off lightly. It says, "Be a different man. Choose wisely. Ahead of you is a Holy City, but just outside it there is the lonely valley of Hinnom."

SEVEN

On Being a Protestant

YOU may have seen the motion picture *Martin Luther*. The climax comes when Luther stands before the Emperor Charles at the Council of Worms in 1521. He has been asked to recant some of the writings he has published during the last four years, writings directed toward establishing what he believed to be "the freedom of the Christian man." He admits that some of his words were written in heat and, knowing Luther, I'm sure they were. But that's as far as he will go. He addresses the Emperor: "My conscience is captive to the word of God. I cannot and I will not recant, for it is neither right nor wise for me to go against my conscience. Here I stand, God helping me, I can do no other." He repeats his last words in Latin for the Emperor's benefit, and then with the graceful salute and bow of a knight he leaves the council chamber, never again to be tried by papal or imperial courts. Carlyle says of that moment: "This was the birth of the modern man."

The drama of Luther's "Here I stand" captivates us all, but what he stood for is often vague and hazy in our own minds. Why am I a Protestant? The easiest and most obvious answer is: "Because my father and mother were Protestants. Let's let it go at that." The only trouble is that you can't let it go at that. Second-hand religion has a strange way of becoming no religion at all. We are told: "He who stands for nothing usually falls for anything." Protestants who have never bothered to learn where they stand usually do fall, and fall for anything, any half-baked religion or semi-religion that comes along.

Of course, some of us will say that Protestantism has nothing positive to stand for anyway; it's essentially negative, isn't it? "Protestant," we think, derives from the verb "to protest." Protestantism by very definition, then, is negative. It's a revolt, a rebellion, of those who do not like the Catholic church, nothing more. I understand that at the recent meetings of the American Dental Association it was pointed out that in America there is a huge increase of teeth-grinding. More and more people in our country won't talk or say what they think; they just go around frustrated, grinding their teeth in anger, or worry, or protest against the way things are going. Well, Protestants have nothing positive to affirm; they are essentially negative; they are against everything; they sit around grinding their teeth.

Actually, nothing could be further from the truth. The very word "Protestant" does not derive from the verb "to protest." It derives from the noun "protestation," a word we seldom use any more. It means: a solemn declaration of fact, opinion, or resolution. You see, when our fathers were first called Protestants at the Diet of Speyer, they weren't thought of as mere rebels against Rome; far from it. The charge was more serious. They were affirmers of a new faith. They weren't just protesting. They were making a solemn declaration of new facts in Christianity. Far from being negative, they were positive, perhaps too positive.

What then do we Protestants affirm? What are the positives in our faith? What do we stand for? To put it more personally, why am I, or why are you, a Protestant?

First of all, *I am a Protestant because I believe that the Holy Bible is the prime rule and guide of my Christian faith and practice.* Ruskin says of the Reformation: "In its right hand there was a Book." Adlai Stevenson says that our fathers built this country with three tools—an ax, a plow, and a book. That book was the Bible.

Now this does not mean, as some think, that we Protestants worship words. That's always the temptation, of course, to make the Bible a book of mottoes, magical sentences, phrases pulled out of context to justify our opinions on slavery, or war, or morals. Word worship, taking the Bible literally, is bad. Even ministers make this mistake. How often we hear sermons about the great heroes of the past on the text from the sixth chapter of Genesis: "There were giants in the earth in those days." But look up the context sometime, see what sort of giants they were, and you will hardly apply those words to any of our forefathers we respected or revered. These holy memorized words have no meaning, you see, without their proper context.

Let's remember, then, that Jesus himself cared so little about exact words that he never wrote anything down. But the spirit behind the words, the spirit of the Bible—that's the important thing, what modern theologians have called "The Word" (capital W) behind the words (small w). This is why I am a Protestant, not because I have a book in my hand that I can quote for mottoes or to win prizes with, but because that book brings the Spirit of the living God closer to my heart and I am able to see my life with a truth and clarity I never had before. Take the Bible seriously, but not literally, and you will be a good Protestant.

Secondly: *I am a Protestant because I believe that as children of God we have direct access to him at all times.* If you want to see the ruler of a foreign country, you have to go to him through his appointed ambassadors: some sections of Christianity believe in the ambassador theory of God. But ours is not such a conception and not such a relation. As a child can go without fear to his father, so may we come to our God, with no intermediary, no appointment, no ecclesiastical authority or official. All are priests before him and every person is the guardian of his own conscience.

This, of course, is both a high and a dangerous doctrine. Protestantism rises or falls with the responsible individual, mind you, the responsible individual. Sometimes we talk about the freedom of the individual and forget his solemn responsibility. But that's far from what the Reformers had in mind. Luther, you recall, made his watchword "the priesthood of every believer."

And what freedom that gave men—men bound in the shackles of priestcraft, men who looked at life much as the young Luther himself did when as a boy he knelt to pray in his church and looked at the stained-glass windows. There was the picture of men drowning in the seas of life, with their arms stretched pitifully out of the black and swirling waters. And through the waters rode a single boat and in it the black-garbed priests, who alone could stretch forth their hands and bring men into the boat and save them. When the mature Luther talked about the priesthood of every believer, he forever cut the shackles of that sort of priestcraft and set men gloriously free. But there's the other solemn half to it, too. Luther never forgot the solemn obligations of a priest, never forgot that he was bound by an awful oath to be faithful to his God. And this is the other half of Protestant doctrine, the half we all too often forget, "every man a priest, every man free before his God." But, oh, the responsibilities of being free! Oh, the sacred obligations of being your own priest before the altar of the living God!

Here is the third reason: *I am a Protestant because I believe that gratitude to God, rather than striving after moral perfection, is the basis of the Christian life.* This is what Paul meant when he said: "The just shall live by faith rather than by works." This is what Luther discovered. For a number of years he was a monk and he was a good monk, observing all the rules that would improve his soul. He did his penance, he observed asceticism, he kept all the letter of the Church law. Then it suddenly dawned on him: "This is not the right way to come to God. This is a dead end, the road of endlessly trying to perfect oneself, to merit heaven, to do bookkeeping before God." "Moral or religious bookkeepers are on the wrong road," he said. No, the Christian man is the man who simply accepts God's love, knowing that he cannot lay moral claim upon God, saying, "I'm this good; you owe me this much." God's love is a gift, not something you merit, or work to secure. You accept God's love by faith, not by works. The essence of your Christian religion is gratitude, not striving after moral perfection.

Many of us as young people have had perfectionist parents. They expected nothing short of the perfect of us—perfect grades, perfect character, perfect preparation for lifework, perfect choice of a wife, perfect success. For a while in our life this was helpful; it made us do our best. We felt: "I must not let Dad down." But there comes a crisis in most of our lives when we feel the tyranny of this perfectionism. It haunts us. It scares us. We get self-centered. We keep saying to ourselves: "Perhaps I won't make it. I got a B in chemistry; I wonder how they'll take that at home." Or "Maybe I won't be the success or the good person they expected." This is not theoretical: half of those who talk to me as a religious counselor or to other counselors on my campus actually suffer from the tyranny of perfection. Now, what's the way out? To strive harder? No. First of all, you've got to say to yourself: "This is a dead end. Striving after perfection defeats itself. I'm not becoming better; I'm just becoming self-centered, self-conscious, self-righteous." Then the second thing is to go home and discover that your dad and mother accept and love you anyway just as they did before. And this is what makes you a truly good young man or woman—the fact that you are accepted regardless of your imperfection and sin, that actually you don't merit love, you receive it.

Protestantism says this about God. You can think of him as the perfectionist father, and then you'll try to merit his favor. But such salvation by works is a dead end. You'll end up under the tyranny of perfection. But if you live by faith, accept the fact that you are accepted, come home, imperfect as you are—then a new peace, and radiance, and freedom come into life. You are a Christian man, you are a good man, no longer because you are a perfectionist, but because you are a grateful man, grateful for love that no man can merit, the love of God himself.

Let me summarize: Why am I a Protestant? Because I believe four things. First, that the Bible, the central message and spirit of the Bible, is the prime rule of my faith. Second, that as children of God we have direct access to him at all times: every man is his own priest. Third, that gratitude to God, rather than striving after moral perfection, is the basis of the Christian life. And finally, *I am a Protestant because I believe that the true unity of the Church comes not through uniformity of organization or institution but through the fellowship of believers.* The Church is united in an organic rather than an organizational sense. When the Catholic speaks of the oneness of the Church he means uniformity under an earthly sovereign; to the Protestant this is not unity but division. The true unity of the Church is a unity of faith in Christ, not of institutional structure. Against this unity, as the Scripture says, "the gates of hell can never prevail."

This kind of unity allows for diversity and permits many patterns of organization. For that very reason it will always appear to be more divided than it really is. But Protestants are not as divided as most people think they are. Protestants believe that in the long run this unity of the Spirit is stronger, more creative than any uniformity of organization, splendid as that may be. There is a strength in elasticity; never forget it. At the turn of the century you may recall that Frank Lloyd Wright was commissioned to build a hotel in Tokyo that would withstand earthquakes. He built it on the principle of elasticity rather than rigidity. Instead of going down to rock he went down to mud and floated its foundation on mud. The walls were not joined but loosely hinged. Only flexible materials were used. He was thought crazy at the time, but when the terrible earthquake struck Tokyo in 1923, devastating the city, the Imperial Hotel alone stood the shock and saved countless lives.

Well, that's our faith as Protestants. The Church that will withstand the shocks of our turbulent civilization must have the strength of elasticity rather than of rigid uniformity. It's a great faith, to be a Christian, and to be a Protestant. I hope that each of you, in the constant and honest searching of his own heart, will come to the place where he can say with Luther: "Here I stand. God helping me, I can do no other."

II.

BRINGING IT HOME TO INDIVIDUALS

EIGHT

To the Lonely

THE world is full of lonely people. A doctor was asked to name the most devastating disease today. His answer was: "Loneliness, just plain loneliness."

Sociologists look at us and call us "the lonely crowd"—a good phrase to describe us, always in a crowd, always surrounded by thousands of others, always so groupy in everything we do, but strangely lonely, pathetically lonely, none the less. Literature goes haywire on this theme. There's Kafka's *Joseph K.,* all alone and accused. There's the atmosphere of separateness and alienation in Beckett's *Waiting for Godot,* or T. S. Eliot's *The Waste Land.* And who has been the hero of the movies for whom we developed a peculiar cult? James Dean, who once said: "I never had the courage to be tender, to relate to another human being." As for students: well, are you free of loneliness? Not really. Only in the picture shows are you the happy carefree crowd, the wholesome American boy or girl meeting life with a large smile, a pigskin in one hand and a Bible in the other. But in actual life you're not as well adjusted as your parents like to think. You, too, are often congested but lonely, in some ways the loneliest generation of youth we've ever had. You see, the language of loneliness is a universal language. We can all understand a bit of it.

In our Scripture Jesus is in the Garden of Gethsemane praying his final prayer before he goes to his trial and death on the Cross. He is surrounded by his disciples but he knows that in a few moments he will be alone. "Behold the hour is now come that ye shall be scattered, every man to his own, and shall leave me alone." He goes on, almost as if it were an afterthought: "And yet I am not alone, because the Father is with me" (John 16:32). This is the language of loneliness, but loneliness that has been conquered.

We might make a distinction to begin with, one which the Scripture suggests. *It's one thing to be alone and quite another thing to be lonely.* Being alone is more or less an accident in life. Everybody leaves for vacation but we live too far away to go home. Or Dad dies and there's an immense hole in the family; a large part of the house is terribly empty now. Or sickness can make us alone. No matter how often our friends come, being in a hospital can be quite a solitary experience. We can be an only child and play alone, or we can be the only Negro in a class of whites, or we can be the only American in a land where everyone else speaks French. Being alone is subject to many a whim of human circumstance and there's often little we can do about it.

But loneliness is quite another matter: it's an inner, spiritual disease. Actually, you can be alone but never lonely, like a woman I buried one cold bleak November morning at a grave far off in the hills of western Massachusetts. Only three of us stood by the grave, myself, the undertaker, and one old friend. But this friend turned to me after the service and said of the lady who had died: "She may have been alone much of her life but she was never lonely." So I believe you can often enough be alone in life but never lonely.

On the other hand, I'm sure many of us can be quite lonely even if we are never alone in life. All your life you've got a crowd around you. Your room is like Grand Central Station at rush hour, your home always has the gang around it. If it ever gets quiet, you can always turn on the radio or the TV and have the intimate company of the Marlboro man with his tattoo. Wonderful, isn't it? You are never alone. But deep down you're quite lonely, surprisingly lonely. And this is the first distinction we all have to make: it's one thing to be alone in life, quite another thing to be lonely. They may or may not go hand in hand. Jesus knew how to be alone, but I don't think Jesus was ever lonely.

Indeed, I'm inclined to think that *the only way you and I can conquer loneliness is to learn to be alone, not less, but more in life*. That may sound like a riddle; it isn't. You see, we all have to face up to what loneliness really is. It's not a geographical accident; it's a disease of the spirit, something that eats away at our souls no matter how many other people may be around us. And the reason why more of us don't conquer loneliness is that we refuse to try to understand what it really is. We dismiss it with geographical excuses: "Everybody must be busy tonight . . . the dating is getting bad around here anyway . . . somebody must have forgotten me. . . ." But that's too easy and we ought to admit it. Being alone does not explain being lonely. And calling in the crowd does not help loneliness; it only aggravates it. Probably the loneliest moments any of us have ever known have been lonely moments in a crowd. So, the solution may be to learn to be alone more just to face up to ourselves. We all have to start there. You may have to be alone more, not less, to conquer your loneliness.

What, then, is loneliness? What is this inner, spiritual disease that is so universal? It has many ingredients but I'll name two I'm sure of.

First of all there's self-pity, a good big block of it, in any lonely person, whether he be elderly or a student such as you may be. Loneliness is 90 per cent self-pity. The victim shuts himself in, others out. Soon everybody avoids him, for nobody loves a self-pitier. See if that isn't right. Next time you suffer from loneliness, ask yourself how much of your loneliness is really self-pity, feeling sorry for yourself. And the sorrier you feel for yourself, the lonelier you grow. You spin your own cocoon.

This is what anyone learns who has had to be alone much in life: watch out for self-pity. I have a friend who was in solitary confinement in prison for two years in Red China. He says that at first he felt sorry for himself. After all, he was only thirty-five years old, he had a family and two youngsters, he had been a good Christian, he had given everything up to serve the Chinese and help them to a better life, he had taken a salary that most of us would have thought insignificant, and now, after all this sacrifice, the Chinese themselves didn't appreciate him, and locked him up without even a trial or any knowledge of the charges against him. "O pity poor me, pity poor me." And as he spun the cocoon of self-pity the lonelier the days became, the more unbearable the slow weeks, until his attitude changed, almost overnight. Instead of asking the question: "Why should this happen to me?" he began asking the question: "Why shouldn't this happen to me?" "After all, I'm a Christian, the Reds are not; it's really a compliment to the work I was doing that they decided to get rid of me. If Christianity is what I believe it is, and if Communism is what I believe it is, then why shouldn't I be in jail?" And the cocoon broke. Far from pitying himself, he felt grateful that God had entrusted to him a witness for his faith among a people who needed that witness. No longer was he lonely even if he was alone. You can track it down every time: the lonely person is the person who has a bad case of self-pity.

And he usually has a bad case of self-sufficiency: that's next. This is what modern art and literature and drama are often talking about, the amazing loneliness of modern man because he clings with an almost heroic tenacity to his own inviolability, his own self-sufficiency. This summer I read what I at first thought was a great book, but later I was not so sure. It's called *Death of a Man,* by Lael Tucker Wertenbaker, whose husband was an editor of *Time* for a while. In July, 1954, he flew from France to New York and learned he had cancer. His wife, against the advice of the physicians, told him the truth. "I cannot lie to this man," she said; "that would take his dignity away from him. He would rather have dignity than hope." Wertenbaker flew back to France, retreated to the hills with his family. There he planned his own death, how he would die with dignity, in control of the situation to the very end. He refused any operations. There was to be no knife work on him. He planned his own allotments of dope, stepping the doses slowly up. Around Christmas he knew the end might be near but he wanted to choose the time. Two nights he took overdoses of morphine, his wife standing by, but the drugs kicked back and he recovered. Then the night after New Year's, after telling his wife how much he loved her, he took the razor from her hands and precisely, deliberately, slashed his wrists and died. This was the "death of a man," as told by his wife, a deeply moving and agonizing story. But when it was all over, as a Christian I couldn't help asking, "Was this really the death of a man? Was this dignity, just to be always in control of the situation, always sufficient to himself, always setting the time, always planning even his end?" I've seen other men die and I thought they had greater dignity. They knew that all men are mortal, that the time of their living and dying is not in their hands, and they died in serenity and faith. But that's the inner tragedy of many lives these days; by mock heroics men try to prove that they are masters of their fates. They talk of dignity but live and die without ultimate dignity, offering the world their pitiful pair of slashed wrists. No, the answer is somewhere else. The free man, the man of dignity, is always the man who acknowledges his proper dependence. He begins with knowing that he is not sufficient of himself. It's the lonely man who insists on being the self-sufficient man.

How, then, do we conquer loneliness? I've suggested that we be alone more, not less. And when we're alone let's face up to the fact that a good deal of our loneliness is a disease of the spirit, of our attitudes. We'll probably find a good bit of self-pity in our hearts, and a good bit of false self-sufficiency. If Jesus kneeling in the Garden of Gethsemane had said: "Buck up, man, you'll make it. Whatever you do on the Cross tomorrow, do it with dignity. Keep your self-control"—I believe he'd have died the loneliest man imaginable. But he didn't take that course. He came at life, at his aloneness, quite another way. What was that other way?

For one thing *he always treated his aloneness as the key or the clue by which he could meet other lonely people.* The strange, inner solitude of Jesus made him the best friend to the friendless. His life is a series of meetings with lonely men and women who were transformed in meeting him. Here is the first clue: treat your loneliness, for we are all lonely in some ways, as an asset, not a liability. There are always right around you others as lonely, or lonelier, than you. And you, in so far as you understand your own loneliness, are the only one who can ever speak an understanding word to them. The only man who helps a lonely person is he who has honestly and intensely known loneliness himself. Loneliness is the key to the heart of many others.

So pick up that key as you go through life. That's the way you'll find your way out of the cocoon of loneliness. Every time you refuse to pick up the key, to share your loneliness, you spin yourself tighter and tighter into your cocoon, even when you're as young as you are. Albert Camus in his novel *The Fall* describes a man who never picked up the key, who made all attempts at love self-love and gradually tightened the threads of his own damnation. Here is the description of the crucial choice he had to make along this line.

I was enjoying my walk. . . . On the bridge I passed behind a figure leaning over the railing and seeming to stare at the river. On closer view I made out a slim young woman dressed in black. The back of her neck, cool and damp between her dark hair and coat collar, stirred me. But I went on after a moment's hesitation. At the end of the bridge I followed the quays toward Saint-Michel, where I lived. I had already gone some fifty yards when I heard the sound—which, despite the distance, seemed dreadfully loud in the midnight silence—of a body striking the water. I stopped short but without turning around. Almost at once I heard a cry, repeated several times, which was going downstream, then it suddenly ceased. I wanted to run but I did not stir. I was trembling. I told myself that I had to be quick and I felt an irresistible weakness steal over me. Too late, too far, I thought, or something of the sort. I was still listening as I stood motionless. Then slowly under the rain I went away. I informed no one.[1]

The whole novel is built around the strange guilt over that incident: a lonely man who at the critical moment could not reach out to another lonely person but under the Paris rain slowly went away.

So one way out is always to treat your loneliness as the real key to another's heart. *Another way, the way of the Christian man, is to be grateful for the love of God.* The way out of the cocoon of self-pity and self-sufficiency is a total orientation of your life in

[1] Albert Camus, *The Fall* (New York: Alfred Knopf, 1957), p. 69.

faith. Jesus had it in the Garden. "They shall all forsake me and leave me alone," he said, "and yet I am not alone, for my Father is with me." Perhaps the reason why so much of modern life is lonely, so much of our own lives, is that we have at the center what the philosophers call "cosmic loneliness." We're never at home in the universe because we have no God to make the universe a home. There's a God-shaped blank in our hearts, and that's why we slash our wrists to plead our own dignity, and why millions of us walk away lonely year after year through the falling rains of Paris, or London, or New York, or Chicago, or even our little town. The truth may be we mortal men are condemned to be lonely, forever condemned, until we find God.

What I'm saying is that the way out of loneliness is real thanksgiving that becomes an attitude of life. No longer "pity poor me"; no longer "life owes me a living"; no longer "I can take care of myself"—you'll walk your lonely path all the rest of your days saying those things. But simple gratitude to God for the goodness and wonder of life will dissolve the cocoon. You may be alone much of your life but you'll never be lonely, for your Father is with you. The stars shine down on you, the sun has a new brightness, the good earth holds you up. God made you, God keeps you, God loves you, God is with you forever—this is the joy of your faith. And you live out your days in gratitude and thanksgiving. A college girl, unknown to me, stood on the walk outside my chapel last spring. The sun was shining, and the whole hillside was covered with pink and white dogwood. All she said was: "It's more than we deserve . . . it's more than we deserve."

> Praise God from whom all blessings flow
> Praise him all creatures here below.

This is the Christian's way out of loneliness.

NINE

To the Organization Man

LET me open with a children's story. If you have had to read a bedtime story to your younger brothers or sisters in recent months you have undoubtedly come across the story of *Tootle the Engine*.[1] It's very popular.

Tootle is a young engine who goes to engine school where two main lessons are taught: stop at a red flag and always stay on the track no matter what. Diligence in these lessons will result in Tootle's growing up to be a big streamliner some day. For a while Tootle is obedient, and then one day he discovers the delight of going off the tracks and smelling flowers in the field. This violation of the rules cannot be kept secret; there are telltale signs in his cowcatcher. Nevertheless, Tootle's play becomes a craving, and despite warnings he continues to go off the tracks and smell flowers. Finally the engine schoolmaster is desperate. He consults the mayor of the town of Engineville in which the school is located; the mayor calls a town meeting and Tootle's failings are discussed, all without Tootle's knowledge. The meeting decides what to do, and the next time Tootle, out for his morning spin alone, goes off

[1] *Tootle the Engine*, text by Gertrude Crampton, summarized by Riesman, Glazer, and Denney in *The Lonely Crowd* (New York: Doubleday Anchor Books, 1954), p. 129.

the track he runs right into a red flag and halts. He turns in
another direction in the field only to encounter another red flag.
Still another, the result is the same. He turns and twists but he
can't find any spot of grass or any patch of pretty flowers in which
a red flag does not spring up, for all the citizens of the town have
co-operated in the lesson. Chastened and bewildered, Tootle looks
toward the track, where the inviting green flag of his teacher gives
him the signal to return. Confused by conditioned reflexes to stop
signs, he is only too glad to use the track and tears happily along
it. He promises never to leave the track again, and he returns to
the roundhouse and is rewarded by the cheers of his teachers and
the citizens of Engineville. He has soon forgotten that he ever
liked flowers anyway. All Tootle remembers is the advice of the
whole world: "Always stay on the track and you will grow up to
be a big streamliner."

Now this innocent piece of moral literature is just right for the
organization man. You can almost hear an executive saying to you
right over his desk, "Stay on the track, Tootle my boy, and you'll
grow up to be a big executive like myself. Whatever you do don't
get out of line. Don't be excessive in anything; always be that man
in the middle. Don't be too brilliant in college; just get along well
with the fellows. Never stick your neck out. Never be different.
Conform to the life around you, never transform it. Don't wander
out in the field; stay right on the track and some day you'll be a
streamliner."

Who is the organization man? What is he like? William H.
Whyte, Jr., editor of *Fortune* magazine, has written a book called
The Organization Man, and I personally would like it to become
the Bible of the campus this year. It holds up a mirror where many
of us can see ourselves right here at college. For the organization
man is not one section of society; he's not the white-collar worker
or the factory man or the professor; he's not a class. He's a spirit;
he's a way of viewing life that has become more and more popular
in modern America. In the old days, Mr. Whyte contends, America
was governed by the Protestant ethic: it stressed individualism,
thrift, competition. But our ethic is changing, he says, to the social
ethic; now the stress is on the group. Individualism and competi-

tion are nasty words. In the old days you used to think of a scientist all alone thinking up great ideas; now the scientist is a team man, working in some highly polished laboratory, doing research for Dupont. In the old days the big business man was the fellow who single-handed took the risks; now the big business man is the man who oils the machinery, keeps all parts of the organization in high gear, and takes few risks personally. In the old days the educated man was the man who was different: he tried to excel in the arts or the sciences; now he's just an average guy in average little suburbia. Something's happened, says Whyte. The gyroscope man, the man inwardly balanced and controlled, is dying off; in his place comes the radar man, always with his tentacles out to feel the pulse of the group and go along with it. This is the organization man. He not only works for big organization; he belongs to it. As one description has it: "These organization men never question the system. They just want to get in there and lubricate it, and make it run better. They are satisfied to be the technicians of society, never the innovators."[2]

If you think this is remote from you, let me bring it home. Those of you who will graduate from college and go into jobs, and even you girls who will marry such fellows, had better take the advice of Tootle the Engine and stay on the track. Conform to the group. Don't stand out, don't be different. The Monsanto Chemical Company, for instance, advertises "No Room for Virtuosos in our Company."[3] The Monsanto people have a film showing the chemists in their company, all in white coats, and the sound track says: "No geniuses there; just a bunch of average Americans working together." The warning is obvious: don't be a genius if you want to work for us. Or there is Sears. Would you ever want to be an executive at Sears? Well, the company has a personality profile of what it wants. You had better rate in the 80th percentile for economics, but don't let your aesthetic sense, your love of beauty, get above 10 per cent. Don't swallow too much of that art stuff in your courses. A man who scores higher than 10 per

[2] W. H. Whyte, *The Organization Man* (Garden City, N.Y.: Doubleday Anchor Books, 1957).
[3] *Ibid.*, p. 238.

cent in aesthetics "accepts artistic beauty and taste as a fundamental standard of life. This is *not* a factor which makes for
executive success. . . . Generally, cultural considerations are not
important to Sears executives, and there is evidence that such
interests are detrimental to success."[4] That's plain enough: fit the
pattern. Or here is a group of GE trainees who were asked what
they would do if a brilliant person like Steinmetz were to apply to
them for a job. A few said that maybe he would work out; because
of the fraternity-like life of the training program they might iron
out his rough spots. Most of them disagreed: the man would be
too hopelessly antisocial to remold. "I don't think we would put
up with a fellow like that now."[5] Well, I could go on: read *The
Organization Man*. If it proves one thing, it is that you boys going
out of college had better always be the man in the middle. Be a
good joiner. Be a good Tootle and don't get off the track.

The spiritual effect of all of this is shocking and here is where
Christianity comes in. Take a look at the organization man on our
campus; take a look at ourselves, for each of us at times thinks and
feels and lives and evaluates like an organization man. He has a
creed with three words in it, and *the first word in that creed is
security*. One recruiter for a corporation came to a university
campus and the first 300 men he interviewed for a job never even
asked about the salary;[6] they talked in terms of the good life, and
every one of them asked about the pension system. Now there's
nothing wrong with pension systems, but when you, the young, ask
no larger questions than that, no questions about what the job is,
the working conditions, the emotional satisfactions within it, the
chance for growth and outreach of your personality—in other
words, if you have no little spark of adventure at graduation, then
the disease is spiritual and we are a civilization walking close to
the edge of inner decay. To bring it home here, when you join a
fraternity or a sorority do you ever ask what its goals are, what it
does? Or do you just want to get in there and be within it, take

4 *Ibid.*, p. 214.
5 *Ibid.*, p. 152.
6 *Ibid.*, p. 77.

out your social insurance for the year, as it were? It makes a difference, spiritually.

The second word in the organization man's creed is *conformity*. "No virtuosos in our company, in our club, in our fraternity, just an average good bunch of guys." So you make sure that everybody is average; you rub off the rough edges of Steinmetz; you shape him up. You remember David Riesman, author of *The Lonely Crowd,* was making a study of comic books. He had an interview with a twelve-year-old girl about her favorite comic. "I like Superman better than the others," she said, "because they can't do what Superman can do. Batman can't fly and that is important." "Would you like to fly?" asked Riesman. "Oh," said the little girl, "I would like to fly if everybody else did, but otherwise it would be rather conspicuous." Well, there we are. The organization man wants your thinking to conform, not just your cashmere sweaters and your white shoes. And believe me, you do conform often enough —we all do. Our model is not the individualist but the well-rounded man. One personnel officer says: "Any progressive employer would look askance at the individualist."[7] Another: "Men of strong personal convictions, willing to make unorthodox decisions, are more frequently given to the characteristics of drive rather than leadership. We used to look primarily for brilliance . . . but now we want a well-rounded person who can handle well-rounded people."[8] You see, organization man is adjustable man—no unorthodox ideas, no radical notions, not too enthusiastic, not too much ambition. In other words, the man who can conform to the organization, be loyal unto the organization "as long as ye both shall live." Young people, always beware of anyone who is constantly talking in terms of loyalty to any group. He is a conformist at heart. Don't fly; you'd be conspicuous, he says.

The third article in the organization man's creed is *compromise* —*yes, moral compromise*. The organization man is always a moral leveler; he cancels out the extremes, the extremely good, the extremely bad. His aim at college is "no conflicts in the house, peace

[7] *Ibid.,* p. 150.
[8] *Ibid.*

and good spirit at any price." And all this is usually sold on the basis that it's a mark of maturity. When you're a "kid" you have ideals, but now you've got to get along with other people, which usually means get along at their level. Again, be that "man in the middle," ethically, morally. And no one ever asks the question: How do you become mature? Could it be that you become mature by being a rugged individualist in your college life, and anyone who doesn't become a bit of an individualist in college is never going to be mature? Could it be that the organization man is permanently immature? Could it be that he's in an ethical fog forever?

Security, conformity, compromise—these are the spiritual marks of the organization man. Now what has Christianity to say? Shall I quote from the New Testament? Jesus said, "You are the salt of the earth; but if salt has lost its taste, how shall its saltness be restored? It is no longer good for anything except to be thrown out and trodden under foot by men" (Matt. 5:13). That's a queer thing to say: Jesus would think the organization man was tasteless, flat, dull, the world's most highly manufactured bore. Or Paul to the Romans said: "Do not be conformed to this world but be transformed by the renewal of your mind . . ." (Rom. 12:2). Come now, Paul, we answer, you'd never get in our fraternity, or our church: we don't want any squares, any people who want to transform the world. Or to the Corinthians: "Are you not behaving like ordinary men?" (I Cor. 3:4). Of course, we protest, we are behaving like ordinary men because we are ordinary men—no geniuses here, no religious geniuses at least, just an average bunch of American guys; don't try any of that hero stuff on me. Or Jesus again: "If any man will come after me, let him deny himself, and take up his cross, and follow me" (Matt. 16:24). Now, Jesus, that's OK for church, but any chap who gets himself crucified is obviously immature. Or there's that young ruler who wanted to be a disciple and Jesus said: "Sell what you possess" (Matt. 19:21). We laugh: "Well, isn't that a bit excessive? I prefer the Gospel of Tootle to the Gospel of Christ."

Let me spell it out. Christians, we all have to live in organizations, big organizations, but we don't have to be organization men. We're not allowed to sell our souls to any group. In the long run we stand before the throne of God as individuals. And there's a place in modern life for the true individualist; there's a place for the Christian nonconformist. How can you be one?

First of all, *you've got to be willing to stand alone at times against your group, even the group you love the most.* And you don't stand alone just to be antisocial; you stand alone because it's the most social thing you can do. The man who loves his group the most is the man who at times stands out alone against the group because of his moral and spiritual convictions. There's a proper loneliness in every Christian.

Secondly, in any group, *as a Christian you'll talk about the goals of the group, not the machinery of keeping the group going.* The organization man is a technician; he doesn't question the system, he just wants to lubricate it. The Christian can develop the skills of getting along, too; he should often be the most sophisticated fellow in the group, rightly sophisticated. But he never isolates his skills of getting along from the why and to what end he is getting along. He demands the purpose of any group and he only joins meaningful groups. He never organizes just for the sake of organizing.

Finally, *I'm sure from what Jesus says that the Christian lives intensively and even excessively in some things.* He's never willing to be just the man in the middle, just average. Jesus said: "Sell all that you have." And he hasn't changed his tune today. He's saying now: "Sell all that you have, young man, young woman, for a few profound convictions about life, what it means and what you're here for. Sell all that you have, bend over backwards, to find one cause of justice and brotherhood to which you can give your heart. Sell all that you have, to think, love and live passionately, intensively, refusing to be just another cipher in the file of some office or the mediocrity of some elegant club. Sell all that you have to be at times a fool and at times a hero for something you believe in, and let the chips fall where they may." The man in the middle never gets into the Kingdom of Heaven; he usually doesn't even know what heaven is like here on earth.

You may be wondering: that will change me quite a bit, won't it? Perhaps it will. A Christian should be somehow different. He should be a New Being. Will any of you, just a few of you, take the chance?

TEN

Always Two Kinds of Hypocrites

No one likes to be called a hypocrite. It's a mean word and it is intended to hurt. Usually people don't say it to us, they just think it, but once in a while they may even tell us. This happened to one student I know. He's a young man who gets up and goes to church on Sunday mornings; most of the other fellows lie around and stay in bed at the fraternity. They call him a hypocrite because he goes. They may have their reasons, I don't know. My guess is they're using the word as it's generally used. They think he's pretending to be better than he really is. This is one good definition of a hypocrite: a hypocrite is a person who pretends to be better than he really is.

Of course, the brothers in the fraternity should understand one thing: there are really two kinds of hypocrites. A hypocrite may be a person who pretends to be better than he really is, but a hypocrite may also be a person who pretends to be worse than he really is. The hypocrite may go to church, yes; but the hypocrite may also be the one lying in bed, the one who's so sure he's not a hypocrite. After all, what does the word "hypocrite" mean? It's a Greek word; it means one who wears a mask, one who's always play-acting as in a Greek drama. So keep your eyes open. All around you are people who wear masks. Some are pious, strait-laced, correct: they're pretenders, pretending to be better than they really are. Others are just the opposite and yet they wear masks too. They're sophisticated, cynical, rebellious, always pretending that they're worse than they really are. You see, there are always two kinds of hypocrites, never one. To use political lingo, some are hypocrites of the right, conservative hypocrites; others are hypocrites of the left, the radicals, the rebellious. In some ways the latter group is more numerous than the former.

Now it's too bad that the Bible doesn't describe both the hypocrite of the right and the hypocrite of the left. In the beginning of his ministry Jesus says to his disciples: "You must not be as the hypocrites are" (Matt. 6:5). Then he describes hypocrites: they are the Pharisees; they stand in the center of the market place when they say their prayers, they give alms ostentatiously, they fast and disfigure their faces. He even tells a parable about two men going up into the temple to pray, the one a Pharisee, the other a publican. The Pharisee stood and prayed thus: "I thank thee, Lord, I am not as other men are, extortioners, unjust, adulterers, or even as this publican. I fast twice in the week, I give tithes of all that I possess." But the publican would not lift up so much as his eyes to heaven but smote upon his breast and said: "God be merciful to me a sinner" (Luke 18:11–13). So goes Jesus' parable. It is aimed at the Pharisee, the hypocrite of the right, the sort of hypocrite Jesus knew and saw and dealt with.

Jesus probably never saw the other type of hypocrite, the person who pretends to be worse than he really is, but if he had I think this is how he would have told that parable. "Two students went to church on Easter Sunday to pray, the one a regular churchgoer and the other a tweedy man of the world. And the man of the world prayed thus with himself: 'God, I thank thee I am not as other men are, simple-minded, superstitious, narrow and inhibited, or even as this poor churchgoer. I get my religion two or three times a year. I give to the charity drives. The rest is wine, women, and song. I may look innocent, but, God, you know me, I get around.' " Well, you can write your own second parable. The point is simple: the sophisticated man of the world is often as much a hypocrite as the Pharisee. And Jesus would look at him, so often pretending to be worse than he really is, and say pointedly: "You must not be as the hypocrites are."

Of course, we should all admit that a certain amount of pretense is necessary to life. There are times when we all have to wear a mask, we have to fit what is expected of us. Psychologists talk about "role playing" and we all do a certain amount of it. In our complicated society I can't see how we can escape. As a class officer you may have to behave at times differently from the way you would as an individual student. You might act one way with the boys at the fraternity and another way in front of your younger brother, and rightfully so. You are probably one type of girl on a date and quite another as hostess at the sorority. You may have to behave one way in an Army uniform and quite another as a civilian. We all have to wear masks at times. Role playing is part of our way of life. But hypocrisy is role playing that has become a fixed trait of character. You can get to the point where you always pretend, either to be better than you really are or to be worse than you really are. And right here Christianity has something to say.

We'll start with *the hypocrite of the right*. We are all that type of hypocrite at times, pretending to be better than we really are. We are all tempted to say with the Pharisee, "I thank God I am not as other men." We have our moral standards and we think they're pretty good. We can say with Booker T. Washington, the great Negro educator, when his fellow Negroes were asking him to start a campaign of hate against the southern whites: "I will let no man drag me down so low." There are times and points at which any self-respecting person will always say: "Here I go and no further. I will let no man drag me down so low." There is a healthy pride in our virtues.

But this healthy pride in our virtues can easily become unhealthy: that's what Christianity reminds us. What is sin for the Christian? Not immorality but pride, pride that makes us independent of God. And there's no pride worse than virtuous pride; we can take anything but that. Mark Twain said of one person: "He was a good man in the worst sense of the word." We've all known such people, good but in the worst sense of the word and, oh, how we avoid them. Some Christians have been described as "starched before they're thoroughly washed."

Or to use another illustration, at the Yale School of Alcoholic Studies one summer a lecture was being given on the detrimental physical effects of alcohol by a distinguished doctor. He recounted the effect on blood pressure, nutrition, brain reaction, and so forth. One lady, who had been nodding assent all through, rose to her feet to ask: "After all you've said, doctor, is there any disease a total abstainer like myself, a non-drinker, could ever get that an alcoholic doesn't?" The doctor thought a minute, then said: "Only one disease, and it's a real bad one. It's called pressure of the halo." And quite simply, this is sin, one of the worst sins, for a Christian. "I am not as other men are." This is virtue that has become pride, starchy virtue.

As you become more mature in the Christian faith you always learn to make the sensitive distinction between righteousness and self-righteousness. In the one you choose goodness for itself; in the other you choose goodness because it makes you more secure and important. This is what the apostle Paul had to say about his own moral experience. In many ways the moral Law of Moses was life-giving for him. He says it was a schoolmaster; it gave discipline and strength and moral integrity. But at a certain point in his life this pursuit of morality went sour. He says the Law began to "work death in me." In other words, his goodness boomeranged; it became psychologically self-destructive. Far from drawing him nearer to God he found that his virtues were keeping him from God. Far from giving him freedom they were just putting him under a new tyranny.

Paul found, what many of us sooner or later find, that it is very difficult to be good without being self-conscious of our goodness, and from being self-conscious we progress to being self-righteous. This seems to be the obsessive logic of the human ego. We men are "the inveterate idolaters"—which means we always figure ways to worship ourselves—and the most subtle and immovable form of self-worship is to worship our own goodness. Righteousness is one thing, but it's a short step to self-righteousness. Goodness is one thing, but starchy goodness, goodness stiffened by pride, is quite another. We are all tempted by goodness in the worst sense of the word.

Remember, then, according to the Christian faith, your virtues can keep you further from God than your vices if they're self-righteously held. This is what Christianity always has to say to hypocrites of the right, those among us who pretend to be better than they really are.

But what about *hypocrites of the left,* those who wear a mask too, pretending to be worse than they really are: has Christianity anything to say to them? I said that according to Christianity the supreme sin is pride. And the sophisticated man of the world has his form of pride, too, which Christianity soon sees through. Listen to his conversation for any length of time. All the way through it, whether he uses the words or not, he will be repeating what Jesus identified as the key to any hypocrite: "I thank God I am not as other men are." "I'm the only free thinker on the block. I'm the only person who's up to date. I'm the one guy who knows the score." This is pride, the worst type of pride in every line, only turned upside down. This fellow doesn't talk about his virtues; he always talks about his vices, but he's just as self-righteous about them as he can be. He's as much a hypocrite as the other. He's always pretending, only this time pretending to be worse than he really is. This is his own form of pride.

Why do we, particularly as young people, pretend to be worse than we really are? I think it's because as young people we easily develop three mistaken notions about life. One is that wrong is somehow more up to date than right; goodness is old fashioned. Another is that wrong is more exciting than right. For the protected adolescent this always looks the case. "Life is not here; it's on the other side of the tracks." Like Jimmy Dean we become a "rebel without a cause," just for kicks. Or perhaps we think that wrongdoing gives us greater freedom than right. It's the only way to become an individual. Underneath everything this is the creed of the sophisticate: he's modern, he's exciting, he's free. This is why he's always pretending.

The Christian answer to such a person is simple: sinners enter the Kingdom of Heaven, but never proud sinners. And the reason?

Because such people ultimately deceive themselves. For after all, what's really up to date? High ethical living, not low. There's nothing new in sin; it is as old as the hills. As for excitement, goodness wins that hands down every time: the first mark of evil is being bored. As for freedom: how do you achieve freedom? By independence and revolt against others? Not at all. Last week on an airplane I met a man who was cheerfully drunk. At times he was funny, but in the two hours I was with that man I learned the other side, the sad and pathetic. What do you think he did just before he got himself drunk? He put through two long-distance telephone calls to his "kids" at college. They cost him eighteen dollars. He wanted to talk, talk to someone he loved. And those youngsters did not even have time to talk to him more than a minute apiece. "Too busy," they said. I'm not blaming anyone. I don't know the whole story. But I do know that the only freedom you'll find in this life is not the freedom to go your own way; it's the freedom to love; anything less than this makes you a neurotic slave. The person who is always talking about his independence is the person who has a thousand secret chains. He deceives himself, says the Scripture.

Hypocrites of the right, hypocrites of the left: we have both among us. We ourselves are often both types of hypocrite: let's not blame the other fellow. We all pretend to be better than we really are, or worse, and the game goes on. How do we get out of it, all this game of pretense?

I believe that the Christian faith helps us all to live beyond and above pretense, beyond and above comparisons with our fellow men. This is the problem of the hypocrite. He lives and judges himself horizontally. And the way out is not more moral gumption, "Christian, Rise and Act Thy Creed," good as that may be. The way out is always a new dimension in life, a different perspective, the vertical coming into the horizontal, God coming into time and making our relationships with our fellow men quite new, seen in a different light, put "under the aspect of the Eternal." Faith gives a man new eyes, for himself and for others. It makes him direct. It makes him sincere. It gives what Paul calls "the simplicity that is in Christ."

This simplicity comes *from seeing ourselves as sinners before God.* The publican prayed: "God be merciful to me a sinner." Our faith says that we are all sinners and come short of the glory of God. And it's this very dimension of depth which makes all pretense unnecessary, all comparisons foolish. It gives what the Scriptures call "truth in the inward parts." You are not the angel you once thought you were. The Christian is no shallow optimist about human nature, including his own. He thinks in depth, he lives in depth. He sees the tragedy of evil and the falsity of much that men call good. He sees himself in a vertical relationship to a holy God, and this very insight undercuts all attempts at hypocrisy. He can no longer live by comparisons.

The Christian faith goes further and says that not only must you accept yourself as a sinner, not only see your life in that dimension of tragic depth, but *you must remember that God in his love accepts you as a sinner.* "God be merciful," said the publican. This is what Leslie Weatherhead calls "the intolerable compliment of God's love." Once you realize that compliment, you no longer live by pretense. The wideness of God's mercy makes that quite impossible. A grateful man simply lives in a dimension beyond hypocrisy, beyond comparisons.

Such a God of mercy and grace is the God revealed in our Lord and Savior Jesus Christ. Before him we need wear no mask. We don't have to prove ourselves. We are not saved by our good works. We don't have to pretend to be better or worse than we really are. God's eyes are always clear and they're the eyes of an infinite, forgiving love, the eyes that watch over a single sparrow in its fall, and never forget that last, lonely, unnamed, wandering child of this earth. The murder of that pathetic five-year-old boy in Philadelphia, whose body was never claimed, never identified, was never solved. Over his tiny grave is a simple marker, giving the date, February 25, 1957, and the words: "Heavenly Father, bless this unknown boy." And it *is* our faith in Christ Jesus that God does bless and remember and love every last unknown one of us. Once you live life in gratitude to such a God, you no longer calculate whether you are better or worse than other men. The root of hypocrisy dissolves in praise. For you the morning stars sing together, and the evening star brings each day a peace this world cannot give or take away.

So I believe that the Christian who knows both the depth of sin and the height of the mercy of God has a certain transparent sincerity about him. The mask is off. He carries no chip on his shoulder. He's got nothing to hide, or prove, or protect. He neither calculates his goodness nor boasts his wickedness. He has that quality of life which someone once ascribed to William James. In his last years at Harvard, James built a house in Concord which had one peculiar architectural feature about it: all the doors and windows were so hinged that they opened toward the countryside roundabout. And a neighbor, observing this, remarked: "That house is just like William James—all the doors and windows of his soul open outward."

This is God's greatest gift to the Christian, the gift of inner simplicity—no more pretense, no more mask. I hope you find it in life.

ELEVEN

To the Egghead

MY SUBJECT is what Christianity has to say to the egghead or intellectual. The term "egghead," of course, came into prominence during a recent presidential campaign. Mr. Stevenson was accused of surrounding himself with eggheads, to which he replied with the clever slogan: "Eggheads of the world unite, you've nothing to lose but your yolks." Using the same term last year at a convocation, a college Dean challenged his audience with the query: "Are you an egghead or a bonehead?" The term, therefore, is relevant: an egghead is an intellectual.

My college campus has quite a few eggheads; at least I hope so. Whether we like it or not, we are all to some extent intellectuals. Education-wise we are in a privileged 10 per cent of the country's population. The average person expects us to use our minds critically and frequently in life, more so than most other people. Perhaps we don't like to be thought too intellectual, particularly if we are women. After all, we are told, no man likes to think that his girl is brighter than he is, so the game is to flatter the boy friend until you have him bagged, and then pull out your Phi Beta Kappa key and give him something to boast about at the office. Anyway, male or female, even when we try to cover up, we are more intellectual than most other folk. We are all eggheads to some extent.

Of course, we are not all eggheads in matters of religion: that's the trouble. The question is: can anyone be intelligent and be a Christian? That's a good question and we often ask it. The answer is at times very disconcerting: there seem to be more boneheads among the Christians on campus than eggheads. And this is even more the case in the world at large. You remember the woman who shook hands with Dr. Coffin in New York City after the morning service and said: "You don't know what a help your sermons have been to my husband ever since he lost his mind." Well, that fits: to lose your mind is a great advantage in religion. Religion is faith, and isn't faith the opposite of reason? Scramble all the eggheads in the world and you wouldn't produce one decent Christian omelet. At least a good bit of the workaday world and the workaday church thinks that way. Across the doors of many a church is the sign: "Egghead, stay out."

Well, what has Christianity to say to you if you are an intellectual? We might start with the New Testament, with Jesus himself. The first commandment is: "Thou shalt love the Lord thy God with all thy heart, and with all thy soul, and with all thy mind, and with all thy strength." (Mark 12:30). It's very interesting to notice that Jesus did not quote the Law of Moses correctly when he cited this commandment. Look up the passage in the sixth chapter of Deuteronomy sometime. It speaks of loving God with all your heart, and soul, and strength—three characteristics. But when Jesus quoted it there was a fourth added, what one scholar has called Jesus' most original contribution to religion: "Thou shalt love the Lord thy God with all thy mind." You can't fully love God if you leave that out: this is the first thing Christianity has to say to you.

What will loving God with all your mind mean? *It will probably mean, for one thing, you'll lose some of your inherited religion.* The mind is a terrible knife; it destroys. But is that so terrible? It may be worth losing a good bit of your religion, in order to find something deeper and better. One of the most important articles in a student's room is a scrap basket, that is, provided he fills it with the right things. Take the average student's desk when he's writing a theme. Here's a typewriter, and here's a scrap basket. And the proof of a good theme is that there is probably more paper in the scrap basket when it's done than there is in or around the typewriter. You see, the process of thinking is always the process of destroying, filling scrap baskets forever and forever. But you destroy in order to produce something of your own, your words, your experience, your theme, your religion. As the Buddhist Scripture puts it: "Those who refuse to discriminate might as well be dead."

So in college you never lose your religion, not in the deepest sense. You pare it down, you discriminate. This is why the mind is so important to Christianity. Really it's not how much you believe that counts; it's how little you believe, but how deeply and personally you believe it. And this is the great advantage the egghead has over the bonehead. Martin Luther said: "Here I stand; I cannot do otherwise." And he couldn't do otherwise because for months on end Martin Luther had thought and thought and thought. He converted himself to Protestantism in a classroom. He had carried out many a scrap basket filled with what had to be discarded. For myself, I can honestly say to you: I wouldn't be a Christian if it weren't for me the most intellectually satisfying interpretation of life I could find. Job once asked: "Shall a man lie for God?" The answer is "No." Not even for God should a man lie to himself or others. When you love God, thou shalt love him with all thy mind.

So the Christian faith encourages the egghead. In our generation we need more Christian eggheads, many more. But Christianity warns the egghead, too. Paul speaks of those who thinking they are wise become fools. These were the Corinthian intellectuals who had just enough philosophy to be arrogant about it. He reminds them: "The foolishness of God is wiser than men." Again, "God hath put to naught the wisdom of men." He makes a realistic appraisal of the Christian movement and says: "Not many wise . . . are called" (I Cor. 1:25, 20, 26). All in all, it is a sharp warning to eggheads, and one that has persisted through the centuries. Mind you, it's not the intellect as such against which this warning is directed; it's the pride of the intellect. The egghead has his own peculiar form of arrogance and for that reason he is often more of a fool than wise.

Now what does Christianity mean by the pride of the intellect? How does it warn you as a growing intellectual? Three ways, I think. First of all, *the egghead can suffer from the pride of narrow abstraction*. This is apparent at college. The egghead, just because he is so logical and bright, can become "gung ho" for one type of thinking and one answer to everything. He chews all the meat off one bone and dogmatically states there is nothing else to eat. The bone may be science: "Science has all the answers to the problems of life; nothing else is relevant; there's only one bone and one meat." Or it may be art: "Theatre is my life." In other words, the intellectual is often the worst type of dogmatist. He abstracts from life its richness and fits everything into his one field of learning.

This is why most of us instinctively distrust the intellectual. This is why the egghead on campus can get such a bad name. We feel he isn't "all there" in spite of his high average, and he may not be. Jesus spoke of religious leaders of his day as "having the key to knowledge but not having entered in themselves" (Luke 11:52). And this is often the egghead. Somehow he knows quite a bit about life but he never seems to enter into it fully. He stands apart; he's always removed, objective, seeing through rather than really seeing. One of his friends said of Lawrence of Arabia, that remarkable but strange hero of the First World War: "He is never alive in what he does." Because he stands aloof from life the egghead is often not quite alive.

So Christianity always warns the egghead: make sure your mind has balance and warmth. Keep it close to life. Indeed, perhaps the most intellectual statement you can ever make is to say that in terms of life there may be limits to the intellect. "There are more things in heaven and earth, Horatio, than are dreamt of in your philosophy." "Christianity is foolishness to those who never ask the questions to which Christ is the answer." The Christian faith rightfully says to the egghead: "Thou shalt love the Lord thy God with all thy mind," but beware of abstraction, the pride of the intellect, the sort of brilliance that only asks one set of questions of life and has neither the balance nor the warmth to see beyond them.

But this pride of the intellect takes another form, according to the Christian faith. *It's apt to make men superstitious.* That may sound odd: after all, the egghead is always the one who claims he has no superstitions but is completely rational in everything he does, the free and independent thinker. Don't be taken in by that. The greatest eggheads of the ancient world that Paul encountered were the Athenians, and you remember along the street, in addition to the altars to other gods, he found one altar to the unknown God, "whom therefore ye ignorantly worship . . ." (Acts 17:23). Just for the fun of it walk along any cultural center in any large city, any street frequented by eggheads, such as Huntington Avenue in Boston, and what do you notice? Right next to the centers of culture are always the parlors of superstition—next to Symphony Hall the palmists, the spiritualist temples, the cults of cosmic healing, the bootstrap religions: it's weird but it's symbolic. Unless he is careful, the egghead can always become a strange combination of reason and superstition. He often has unknown gods he ignorantly worships.

Remember, then, there are superstitions of the irreligious as well as the religious: indeed, at times the former seem to have more superstitions. Actually, there is nothing more pathetic than the snob intellectual who gets talking about Christianity and does nothing but reveal his abysmal ignorance in every other statement. More eggheads are real boneheads in matters of religion than in any other field I know and we might as well call a spade a spade. I'm amazed at some of the superstitions of the irreligious I've had to listen to on my college campus. Superstition number one: "Religion is always an escape mechanism." My word, have these eggheads ever read the lives of the saints or listened to the prophets of Israel? Superstition number two: "Missions are a form of Western imperialism and we should leave the happy natives alone." Well, why not make an empirical study of the happy natives for once and realize how unhappy many of these so-called happy ones are? And then why not face the truth that white men compose less than 10 per cent of the mission movement and haven't held leadership positions for years? Superstition number three: "Religious thought never changes; the Church is always in status quo." I've heard the most intelligent men on campus discuss Christianity as if it were still the religion of their boyhood. They don't even seem to know they're talking about something that hardly even exists any longer. They're kicking a corpse. Then there is that old Superstition: "Religion is always at odds with science." You wonder if eggheads don't know that that battle was largely fought before the 1930's and that there have been such religious scientists as Albert Einstein. I could go on. The whole point can be put simply: just because a person is an egghead in some area, he may be far from an egghead in matters of religion. Indeed, he may live in a world of plain superstition, the superstition of the irreligious.

The pride of the intellect takes another form which Christianity warns us of: *a certain cynicism toward other people.* So often the egghead, the intellectual, is a person who uses his brains to cut other people down—down to size, he says. You can always use your mind as a club, to beat other people into submission to your ego. This is why Paul said: "Knowledge puffeth up" (I Cor. 8:1). It does with some people. This is why Jesus said: "Judge not, that ye be not judged" (Matt. 7:1), by which he didn't mean you shouldn't be critical, because a critical mind is the very essence of education. What he meant by judgment was the sort of judgment that calls another person "thou fool." This is the sort of judgment that boomerangs on the judger, the pride of the intellect that makes us cynical toward others.

Here is the final test of the real intellectual: can you have a brilliant mind without hurting everyone around you? Can you have strength without making everyone else weak? Does your mind encourage others to think or discourage them from it? In other words, does thinking make you love your fellow men the more or make you hate and distrust them? This is the egghead's choice and it's all-important.

What then has Christianity to say to the campus intellectual? "Come on in. No one can love God unless he loves him with all his mind as well as his soul and strength. We need not fewer but more intellectuals in the Church." But even as Christianity extends that invitation it warns us against certain prides of the intellect, certain egghead sins: the sin of narrow abstraction, producing its own egghead form of dogma, the sin of superstition, of unknown gods ignorantly worshiped, the sin of cynicism toward others, the mind without love, a terrible thing.

But if such a mind is terrible, I should close by saying it's wonderful to have a dedicated mind, a mind that is penetrating and critical but at the same time close to life, sensitive and balanced; a mind that has its own blend of faith and reason, what the saints used to call "the intellectual love of God"; a mind that is both sharp and kind, that judges in charity and yet is never sentimental; a mind that knows the limits of mind, that knows, as Pascal once put it: "The heart has reasons that the reason knows nothing of"; a mind that explores with daring the secrets of nature and yet is aware that all of nature is surrounded by mystery, endless star-studded mystery; a mind that never blunts its growing edge or loses its childlike wonder at something new. To offer this to your Creator is the perfect gift. To refuse it to him is a tragedy beyond description.

TWELVE

To the Amateur Psychologist

THE question before us is: What has Christianity to say to the amateur psychologist among us? You notice I use the word "amateur." I presume that the mature psychologist is one who knows the limits of psychology, of all science for that matter. He never lets psychology or science become a religion; hence he has no conflict with the Christian faith.

But the amateur psychologist, the student psychologist, is often quite another story. He worships psychology. It is the new answer to every problem. Perhaps he starts with the white rat, but he soon ends up with the science of conditioning; from the science of conditioning he goes to human engineering; from human engineering to human predictability; from predictability to some sort of scientific utopia. Or the amateur psychologist among us may have read Freud and he's now an analyst of some sort. He always gives you that "knowing" look, that psychological eye. There's always that inquisitive probing question: "So you never got along with your father?" Or, "Do you have any hidden hostilities?" Or, "Have you been dreaming of antelope recently?" Let's admit it: This is "the psychological age"; we're all interested in what's going on inside our minds and in other people's, too. We're all amateur psychologists to some extent, and as amateurs we're apt to make mistakes that the wise never do. We're apt to draw conclusions, think we have all the answers to the human problem. In other words, we're likely to lose sight of psychology as a legitimate science and put our faith in psychology as a religion. Here is the problem, here is the conflict with Christianity. Christianity is concerned with faith, and psychology among amateurs can often become a rival faith.

Let me spell it out, this faith of the amateur psychologist, this new religion he's found. There's ingredient number one: *he's a firm believer in manipulation of people,* subtle manipulation perhaps, but manipulation nevertheless. "Why study psychology if you can't manipulate people?" he says. And manipulate them for their own good—he's sure of that. You recall what Henry David Thoreau once said: "Whenever you meet someone who wants to do something for your good, always run from him as fast as you can." Well, the amateur psychologist tends to be fascinated by his "techniques of control."

If you don't think this is the case, sit down sometime and find out why so many students take psychology in college. They take psychology to learn how to "handle people better." What do they mean? They mean that when they get into father's business they'll be able to take over labor relations—handle the worker for the good of the company, make him feel happy. Or they mean handle the customer—what is the psychology that makes him buy or not buy? Or they mean handle personnel—iron out human relations so that the machine keeps well oiled and in highest gear. There's nothing wrong with this ambition as such, at least not right off. But notice the purpose. This has been called "the age of manipulation" and the amateur in psychology is always fascinated by that characteristic of his age. He wants the clue to handling people.

This craving to manipulate comes to its sharpest and most frightening focus, no doubt, in the modern application of psychology to advertising. Did you read about the theater in New Jersey that hired the Subliminal Projection Company to increase its sale of food and drinks at its stand in the lobby? In between flashes of the movie, without anybody's knowing it, at 1/3000 of a second, ads were flashed on the screen. Mind you, they were so fast the eye couldn't see them, but the subconscious could. And in six weeks the sale of Coca Cola increased 18 per cent and of popcorn 57 per cent. How delightful; what infinite possibilities that offers! In the middle of the movies on Friday nights we preachers could flash lovely pictures of a church with mottoes "Go to Church and Find Peace of Mind"—all without your knowing it. You could become Christian by intravenous feeding, by subliminal projection.

Indeed, if Vance Packard is right in his book *The Hidden Persuaders,* there is a real menace to the way psychological manipulators have been linked up with the advertising game these days. Take a look at your ads. What do they tell you about the product itself? Almost nothing. But they create a symbol, a picture in front of you; they play upon your fears or tensions. Here is a car ad. Does it talk about the machine? No, or if it does only in fine print. All the ad says is "It makes you feel like the man you are." Ego-satisfaction—that's the line. Or if you want to sell soap, don't say it makes you clean, but it makes you beautiful. (Cosmetic manufacturers found this out: "We don't sell soap any more, we sell hope"—to women who think they're losing their beauty.) If you want to sell home freezers, appeal to emotional security: your home freezer is bountiful mother. If you want to sell an election, don't discuss issues, keep smiling, look confident. You get the point. This is the age of psychological manipulation, so much so that even the founders of Motivation Research (for that's what this alliance of advertising with psychology is called) are worried. Their own magazine editor says: "One of the fundamental considerations involved here is the right to manipulate human personality." Well, that *is* it, the whole problem of psychology sold as a faith. How far can you manipulate personality? Are there any limits to your right to "handle" people, even for their own good?

The amateur psychologist not only believes in manipulation (that's ingredient number one in his creed), *he's usually also a firm believer that moral and spiritual values are "purely relative,"* by which he means that they have no ultimate significance in the universe; they are just a matter of personal taste or perhaps personal adjustment to a certain environment. The value of psychology for the amateur and for many a student is to help him get rid of guilt, get rid of his conscience. After all, conscience is a super-ego of some sort, a repressive and authoritarian force that the educated person gets rid of. Nothing is really wrong with you that a bit of adjustment of your inner gears can't fix. This is the way he's apt to think.

Now, mind you, this is not what a mature psychologist will ever say. Guilt, he knows, is part of any sensitive and creative personality; a man without guilt is bordering on the neurotic as much as is a man with morbid or excessive guilt. But the amateur jumps the gun. With the permission of psychology, or what he thinks is psychology, he kicks himself free. And a good bit of psychology seems to endorse this basic indifference to moral or spiritual values, After all, what is religion for Freud? Apparently "The Future of an Illusion." What is the faith of his fathers, the Jewish faith? A bad-conscience reaction over the killing of a tribal leader, Moses. Or in *Walden Two,* by B. F. Skinner, the brave new world of some behaviorists, how is religion treated? The local clergy are invited into the colony once a year to distribute charity. This practice is hardly very significant. To the amateur it all adds up: psychology disposes of moral and spiritual values. Religion is an illusion, or a tribal custom, or an arbitrary super-ego. It's at best a harmless pastime.

There's a third article to the creed of the amateur psychologist. *He believes that man can remake man without any help from God.* He's a humanist, in other words. All we men need is the right set of tools, and like God we can create a new man. In the recent Broadway musical, *Li'l Abner* there is a catchy mambo number called "O Happy Day" which satirizes this utopian dream:

> O happy day when miracles take place
> And scientists control the human race.
> When we assume authority of human chromosomes
> And assembly line women, conveyor belt men,
> Settle down in push button homes.
> O happy day when in collective brains
> No individuality remains.
> We'll be a race of busy bees in happy honeycombs. . . .

So much of this, so much of that for ears and eyes
So much of this, so much of that for toes and thighs.
Pour in the pot, stir up the lot, that's the basic plan
What have we got, I'll tell you what, we've got man-made man.

That's humanism defined. Scratch any amateur psychologist deep enough and you'll find down underneath the utopian dream of "man-made man." That's not his science, that's his faith. He's got a religion, a new religion, although he would never call it that, a religion without any living or significant God.

These are the ingredients, then, of the faith of the amateur psychologist among us: manipulation of people for their own good, moral indifference or relativism, and the humanist hope of man-made man. What has Christianity to say to this rival faith on campus? What does it mean to be a psychologist, a true behavioral scientist, and yet be a Christian?

For one thing, *a Christian student of psychology is one who takes seriously the integrity and dignity of every human being.* "God created man in his own image, in the image of God created he him" (Gen. 1:27). There may be some disagreement as to what we mean by the image of God in every man. For some it would be his reason, as in Hamlet's lines on man: "What a piece of work is man, how noble in reason, how infinite in faculties, . . . how like a god. . . ." For others it would be his self or his soul, though soul is certainly a much abused and slippery word, even for Christians. For others it would be his capacity for freedom, his moral sense and his responsibility—this is his image of God. Whatever it is, for the Christian every man has his own God-given integrity, his own creative mystery, if you please, which can be manipulated and controlled and brain-washed only so far and no further. The difference between an amateur and a Christian psychologist probably lies in how much he is aware of the mystery of every person, the image of the Eternal in every man.

Actually, Christianity teaches us not how to handle people but how to love them. Will Rogers once said: "I never met a human being I couldn't love." This is the real reason for the study of psychology by the average Christian: to widen his areas of understanding and love. Manipulation, even for a person's own good, is not love and never can be. This is not to say that we humans are not often machinelike and conditioned. I have a friend who was in the Navy during the last war. A bomb struck, the oil was set on fire, and two of his buddies were trapped in the hold. He was the first to get to them, and there they were, black and curled up like a foetus in the womb of a mother. To this day the awful thought haunts my friend—that human life is "the uncurling from one womb only at last to curl back into another in death." Well, in one way it is, but that's not all of it for the Christian. The image of God is in every man, and the machine of our body or mind never tells the whole story. For that reason there are limits to manipulation which every Christian psychologist will respect.

Then, *the Christian psychology student is certainly one who believes that moral and spiritual values are critical and central to any person.* This does not mean that one particular morality is final or ultimate—not at all. The Christian faith, so far as I can make it out, has no final moral code and laws: morality is always relative in that sense, always conditioned by time and place in history. But that's a far cry from moral indifference. The Book of Genesis says of Noah: "Noah was a just man in his generation" (Gen. 6:9). Notice, in *his* generation he was good, not in yours or mine. Goodness may be described in many different ways in our separate generations. But the ultimate concern of Noah for goodness makes him one with good men of every time and generation. So, psychology may reveal much that is trivial and transient and silly in our consciences: that's its job, its God-given job. But it never destroys conscience as such. To say that morality is relative is never to say that morality is unimportant. Toynbee's judgment of every civilization is that it is a scaffolding around a central tower. What is the tower? Its morality and religion. And what's true of civilizations is true of persons. Religion is more than the "future of an illusion," far more.

Finally, I'm sure the Christian student of psychology not only draws limits to human manipulation, the limits of love; and not only takes seriously the moral and spiritual quest of every person he meets; *he also places his faith in God-made man rather than man-made man.* In other words, the grace and love of God are a factor in the healing of any of our minds or broken emotions or fears or hostilities or conflicts. This is the meaning of many of Jesus' healing miracles. Remember the wild Gerasene boy in the Scripture. When he was healed, he was made one, he was integrated. And Jesus said to him: "Return . . . and show how great things God hath done unto thee" (Luke 8:39). Our Christian faith believes that healing of the mind, as well as of the body, is the work of God. God remakes man—not you, not me.

There's a phrase professional psychologists and counselors always use: "I don't want to play God." The reason why it is used so often is that it's probably our greatest temptation in psychology, just to play God. Sin for the Christian, the supreme sin, is pride, putting yourself in the center, not God. And this is just what the amateur psychologist often does. Think of the Oberlin professor who one day announced to a bewildered student: "There is no God, and I'm his prophet." That's an inevitable sequence. I have never yet met a person who got rid of God who didn't in one form or another put himself in his place—"I am his prophet." This is psychology without a sense of sin, a sense of sin in the psychologist himself. For the Christian this is "the outer darkness," the spiritual death of the man who is always playing God.

But we should end on a more positive note. Can't we say that the intense and passionate search for the self, which is psychology in its greatest height and depth, actually becomes and parallels the search for God? At least this is the Christian's firm faith. There's a new world opening in our time, a world in which psychology and religion are talking much the same language and talking to each other as never before. When Karen Horney, the renowned psychiatrist, died a few years ago, it was Paul Tillich, a Christian theologian, who gave the address at her funeral service. I close with his words. "She was a professional psychiatrist, but she became more and more aware that you cannot listen intensively to people who speak to you, that you cannot listen even to yourself, if you do not listen to the voices through which the eternal speaks to each of us."

THIRTEEN

To the Person Who Never Has Had a Religious Experience

I WANT to talk to the young person who honestly feels that he's never had a religious experience. He's a decent sort of fellow, she's a decent sort of girl, but this person has never been "shook up," as we say, by religion and he's honest to admit it. I met a young man this summer who almost came to my college. He didn't because of a question on one of the admission blanks at that time: "Have you ever had a religious experience?" It's not on the blanks now, nor has it been for a number of years. But he didn't know how to answer it. It's like the question "Have you ever fallen in love?" You might say yes, you might say no, depending on what you mean.

Then there's the daughter of a professor I know. While she's in college her roommate suddenly gets religion. Things change. The roommate gives up some of the things she used to do; she seems to have a certain peace of mind she didn't have before and a lot of conviction. Whether you agree with her or not, something obviously has happened to her. And the professor's daughter, who all her life has been a nominal Christian, comes and asks: "Why doesn't it happen to me? If Christianity is all you say it is, then why doesn't it ever seem to hit me, shake me up?" This is a good, clean, honest question from the heart.

I know some of you feel the same way about your Church. You're not smart alecks, you've got nothing against religion really: "The music's good, the preacher's not a bad guy, a lot of kids seem to get something out of it, I'll get my credit." "But," you go on to admit rather wistfully, "nothing ever happens there in church, nothing happens to me." You wonder why. You've a right to wonder why.

Why doesn't religion shake some of us up? The easy answer, of course, is just to say *religion is a mystery, a complete mystery.* Jesus said: "The wind bloweth where it listeth, and thou . . . canst not tell whence it cometh, and whither it goeth: so is every one that is born of the Spirit" (John 3:8), everyone who is spiritual. You see, Jesus is saying: religion is like the wind, rather capricious. It blows on some, it doesn't blow on others. Some people have religion, some don't. It's a mystery.

Or it's like the story of Paul's religious experience on the road to Damascus. He saw light in heaven, he heard voices, he talked to Jesus, he fell to the ground, he was led blind into the city, he was converted. But what about the fellows who were with him on that journey? The Bible says, in Acts 22:9, that the men who were with Paul saw the light but did not hear the voice of the one who was speaking to him. Here they were in the very same spot on earth as he was, but nothing happened. Paul was shaken; he went to the ends of the earth preaching what had happened. But they went about their business as usual as if nothing had ever happened. It's a mystery.

Perhaps you might say religion is something like music. Some people are tone-deaf, like a girl I once took to hear the Boston Symphony Orchestra. After the concert her only remark was: "It gives me a headache to see so many men work so hard." Rhythm and color and sound were wasted on her. So, most deep experiences of human life are fundamentally mysterious. They happen to some, they don't happen to others. Some of us may be religion-deaf.

Well, we can all admit that there is plenty of mystery in religion; it's a mysterious thing we do in church, worship the invisible. I never cease to wonder at it. But saying something is mysterious and letting it go at that is simply too easy. Our job in life is to admit mystery, but we must learn to co-operate with it. Jesus said that the spiritual life is like the wind, but when we go sailing in the summer in Maine we don't just sit by and accept the mystery of the wind, now northeast, now southwest. We channel the mystery of the wind; we change with it, adjust the sail, steer where the wind is likely to be blowing. So, just to say that the spiritual life is all mystery is to throw in the sponge too soon, evade the question. It's good for lazy landlubbers; it's not enough for sailors.

Let's tackle it then: What has Christianity to say to the person among us who admits religion never shook him up, who asks, often pathetically: "Why does it happen to others but never to me?"

Briefly I'll suggest three answers by way of three questions we might ask ourselves. The first is: *Am I thinking too much in terms of a stereotyped religious experience?* In other words, when we talk about religious experience do we always think of it in terms of Paul, or our parents, or the man who got converted in the Billy Graham meetings in New York, or the college student who reads the Bible two hours every day and suddenly gets religion? Have we only one picture of religious experience in our minds and then when nothing happens to us *of that type* we say we are religion-deaf?

This is where a lot of college talk about religion goes wrong. Listen to any student talking about how he has no religion and you'll find out sooner or later he has a very narrow idea of what religion really is. He's thinking in terms of how other people have experienced religion and he says it's not for him. Of course it's not for him; it never should be. Recently I stood on Times Square. On every corner there was an evangelist of some sort, each holding an American flag, because the New York law is that you can hold a street meeting if you hang on to an American flag—then the police will protect you. So I spent two hours making the rounds of six meetings. In a way I admire those people. I'd never have the nerve to preach on Times Square. But I noticed two things about all of them. They had no sense of humor, and each of them had one answer for being a Christian, one way and only one to be converted. And that one way to Christ was obviously not for me.

Remember, according to the Christian faith, there is no such thing as one religious type or one religious experience. God is strictly informal. He comes to some of us when we are alone, to some when we are with a group. He comes to some when they are sad, and others making merry; to some as a vision, to others as a cup of cold water given to a child in need. And don't ever put God in a dress suit. Don't ever say he can only meet me in such and such a way and on a particular occasion. Are you concerned that religion has never happened to you? Perhaps it has, but in your own way, and you are thinking of it in terms of someone else's experience which cannot and never will be yours.

A second question you might ask yourself is: When I talk about a religious experience *am I always thinking of something emotional rather than intellectual?* Now religion is emotional, of course; who would want it otherwise? But I'm willing to say that real religion is as much intellectual as it is emotional. As a matter of fact, I'll go further and say that if Christianity is never intellectual to you, if it never hits you as the most logical and magnificent truth about life you'll ever find, then it's pretty second-rate Christianity and you won't keep it long. Jesus said: "Thou shalt love the Lord thy God with all thy . . . mind" (Luke 10:27).

Indeed, I'm willing to guess that, while you're in college, and even after you get out of college, your real religious experiences will be intellectual experiences. Never underestimate "the intellectual love of God," as the saints have called it. Thomas Aquinas, the great Catholic thinker, had an experience of God while writing a book; Albert Einstein, while working out a long mathematical equation. Albert Schweitzer admits he owes it to thinking that he was able to retain his faith. And did you ever read the story of Judge Medina, the New York judge who went through the long weary months of trying those eleven Communists, with every kind of pressure on him from the left and the right? He says, "I was ready to give up; I went to my chambers, just thinking as hard as I could over all the details of the law, when suddenly I had an honest realization that God was near. Nothing strange, nothing supernatural, I'm not a mystical person. But I went back to my court and the trial, because now I knew that someone was with me all the way." So, don't expect a religious experience in some far-off emotional way, some escape from ordinary college life. Honest pursuit of the truth right where you are —writing a theme, working an equation, performing an experiment, working out the details of the law—may bring you closer to God, to a God who wants us to love him with all our minds, to that "someone else who is with us all the way."

Third: if you feel that religion happens to other people but never to you, you might honestly ask yourself: *Do I ever give religion any sort of break in my life?* I mean: Do you ever discipline your life, ever deny yourself anything to make some room for religious truth and insight to come to you? Jesus says: "Ask, and it shall be given you; seek, and ye shall find; knock, and it shall be opened unto you" (Matt. 7:7). But in the language of the New Testament those verbs are intensive: they mean keep on asking, keep on seeking, keep on knocking. Religion is never a one-shot proposition, never for the soft and lazy, never offhand. God comes to those who make room for God, those who give the things of the spirit a real break in their lives.

This may mean going to church, your own church: I hope it does. But if not that, I'm sure it means at least two forms of discipline while in college. There will need to be *the discipline of solitude,* getting off alone a few minutes each day, however you can manage it. Recently the newspapers carried the story of John Gormley, a young fellow in San Diego who was found perched one afternoon on top of a 140-foot hospital chimney. When the police coaxed him down and asked what he was doing there, all he would admit was that "he wanted to get away from people." Ridiculous as that was, there will be times when all of us wish we could climb to some place to do the same, because without solitude, some time alone each day, the big, ultimate questions are never asked. Religion is still, as Whitehead remarked, "what a man does with his solitariness." It takes discipline to be alone and like it.

And with the discipline of solitude there comes another discipline, which, for want of a better term, I would call *the discipline of openness*. Train your mind and heart to be receptive, sensitive, aware, during your college years. These are the best years for openness in every area—openness to beauty, to love, to truth, to the Eternal. If you don't cultivate receptivity now, you go out and, with or without your degree, you join the ranks of the living dead. As T. S. Eliot describes the commuters on a foggy morning going to work in London, heads down, without imagination, just doing the job: "I never knew that death had undone so many." Or to use an illustration from a science book I was reading the other day. It described children lost in the forest and raised as animals: a number of such cases have been recorded. The terrible thing is that, when these children have been brought back to civilization, have been given food and shelter, have been placed in schools and loved, the most any of them ever managed was a few words and acts and then slowly they died, because, and simply because, as the article stated, "they had lost the power of relating themselves to human love and once that has been lost it can never be repaired." So the ability to respond, to relate yourself to the Eternal isn't yours forever. Now is the day to be sensitive and open to the things of the spirit. Now is the day that may never quite come again.

I hope, through training yourself to be alone and to be receptive, you will grow spiritually and have your own religious experience in college. Religion is a mystery, yes, but it can happen to you—if you don't always try to think of religious experience in terms of someone else's experience, and if you don't always confine it to something emotional rather than intellectual, and if you are willing to assume some of the discipline of the spiritual life.

Kierkegaard once said, "Every generation must face Jesus Christ anew." Christ is the same "yesterday, today and forever." But to each of us he is the Eternal Contemporary, ever different, ever new.

FOURTEEN

When We Are Tempted

THERE are many things you may question about the Book of Genesis, but one thing seems sure: the writer or writers certainly knew people. Take those first few chapters of Genesis, for instance. What strikes us right off is how little space the author leaves between the story of creation and the story of temptation. Listen to Chapter 1: "So God created man in his image, in the image of God created he him." Then turn to Chapter 3 and what do you find? "And when the woman saw that the tree was good for food [that's understandable], and that it was pleasant to the eyes [she was aesthetic], and a tree to be desired to make one wise [by this time poor Eve had convinced herself that she would suffer a 'cultural lag' if she didn't eat that apple] and that it was in the midst of the garden [you see, that tempting tree was right smack in the center of her life, she couldn't escape its fascination], she took of the fruit thereof, . . . and gave also unto her husband . . . and he did eat." And the conclusion of the tale is: Eve became "the mother of all living." That's it, the picture this ancient writer had of the average human life, each of our lives. Our first experience is to be born, to be created. But we don't go far from the cradle before we have a second and equally important experience: choosing between right and wrong. It's a pattern as old as the Garden of Eden: Chapter 1, creation; Chapter 3, temptation.

Now in discussing temptation there are two things we should get clear right off. One is that *temptation is on all different levels of life:* it isn't confined to sex, or to drinking, or to the young or the old, the educated or the uneducated. Sometimes we hear people say, "I'm too old to be tempted," like the rhyme:

King Solomon and King David lived merry, merry lives
With their many, many lady friends and many, many wives
Till old age crept over them and then with many qualms
King Solomon wrote the Proverbs and King David wrote the Psalms.

Well, we may wish that as we get older we will naturally escape moral choices, but it simply isn't true. No matter how old or good you get, you'll never reach the point where all you'll do is write proverbs and psalms. Nor will you ever be able to confine temptation to one area of your life—it will always threaten. There are childish levels of temptation, there are the levels of the flesh, there are the temptations of temperament, there are the temptations of the spirit and all the agonies involved. No one can tell you what your temptation will be; all we can say is that you will be tempted, and on many levels of life. Temptation cannot be confined to one age or one area.

Then we should go on and say that *temptation isn't the whole problem of morality; it's really the second half.* The first half for many people is the problem of moral insight. Temptation implies that you see a choice, that there is a reasonably obvious and dramatic contrast between black and white. If the whole world is a dull gray and there are no meaningful choices of good or evil, then there simply are no temptations. What I'm getting at is that in every moral situation you first have to see the choice and then you must have the power to choose, but seeing the choice is presupposed. And here is where many of us moderns are lacking. Theodore Dreiser speaks of Sister Carrie as having "an average little conscience"—no moral struggle, just drifting day by day, no real choices, just average and just little. What a contrast to the classical temptations of St. Anthony or Martin Luther! At least they were dramatic. They saw devils, they fought with demons, they knew what was right; their problem was to choose the right and do it. But for many of us there are no devils and no saints, and life has no moral bang to it; it tends to be a quiet, sad whimper. So the first problem is honestly to see the choice. You are to be congratulated if you are tempted; it means you have moral insight. It is at that point the second problem comes in: having seen the choice, how do you find the power to choose the right over the wrong, the better over the poorer, the higher over the lower? And this second problem is what is involved in temptation.

But once this has been said, the question for many of us, all of us, still is: when we are tempted how can we win, how can we come out on top? Out of moral conflict and choice how can we achieve victory? The best answer I know is found in one verse of the tenth chapter of Paul's first letter to the Corinthians; it's worth memorizing: "There hath no temptation taken you but such as is common to man, but God is faithful, who will not suffer you to be tempted above that ye are able, but will with the temptation also make a way to escape." Paul was talking to people who had to make moral choices every day; the contrast between pagan and Christian was dramatically obvious. Theirs wasn't so much the problem of moral insight but finding the power to choose the best, having seen it. And in this single verse Paul gives them, and us, the answer. He indicates the way to face our temptations and win a victory for Christ.

Notice first of all: Paul suggests that *when you're tempted don't regard yourself as an exceptional case.* "There hath no temptation taken you but such as is common to man"; say that to yourself. For whenever you and I are in a situation where we have to make a moral choice, what are we inclined to do? Just make exceptions of ourselves. This situation is different—that's always the subtle psychology of temptation, isn't it? This is uncommon to man; no one ever faced this sort of problem before. "Oh, under ordinary circumstances a man shouldn't cheat, or steal, of course not. But this is different: business is business and everybody's doing it." Or we say: "Under ordinary circumstances a man shouldn't get drunk. But this is different: after all, the club only gets together once a year, you know." Or again: "Thou shalt not commit adultery: that's a good solid commandment. But our problem is unique: my boy friend never had a happy home life, and no one understands the pressures we are under, and I wouldn't be surprised if I had an overactive libido." So it goes. Put this down in your book: every sin is prefaced with the three words "I'm an exception." Remember the little girl who was rebuked for swearing? When she said she had learned it from daddy, her mother answered: "Well, daddy is daddy." To which the little girl replied: "Well, I'm I'm."

I suppose this is one of many reasons why those cadets at West Point a number of years ago made their much-publicized mistake. One West Point graduate wrote a letter: "Actually I believe that the honor system began being pulled away from the cadets ten years ago. It was then that a high salaried civilian football coach was hired. He was and is a man of obvious integrity. But his natural and primary interest was the development of a team. When he arrived we were an average bunch, myself included. Our lives were the same as those of all other cadets. But then came changes. Special seminars were conducted by faculty members for football players, practice periods became longer. Football players became more and more separate from the corps of cadets. It was soon easy to think we were exceptions to the rule." That's not the whole story, of course, but it's at least an honest confession of how one man found it. Temptation came by being made an exception.

That's why Paul so wisely reminds us that when we face temptation we should always start by saying to ourselves, "This is old stuff; this is common to man. Whatever I do I'm not different." This is how Jesus overcame his temptations. All the devil tried to do was to convince Jesus he was different. "Command these stones to be made bread," he said, but under his breath: "Other people, of course, can't do this, but you're different." Or, "Cast yourself down from the pinnacle of the temple. Others can't do that but you're God's darling: the rules don't apply to you." Or, "Bow down and worship me. Of course, I know that's forbidden by God, but he'll make an exception in your case; think of all the good you can do with my armies at your back." And what was our

Lord's reply every time? Just the oldest words of Scripture he could find, what God said back there to Abraham, or Moses, or David, or Isaiah. "I'm not different; what you're tempting me with is as old as the hills," said Jesus. And without that same attitude we can never conquer temptation. Not "I'm I'm," but "There hath no temptation taken you but such as is common to man."

Paul goes further: he suggests, *when you're tempted always remind yourself that you are never alone in your temptation.* "God is faithful," he says. "God stands by, and because he does, you can win. You will never be tempted above that ye are able." Remember, Christian, in the hour of moral trial you are never alone.

Indeed, not only God stands by you but so do all God-fearing and God-loving men and women you have known, says the New Testament. There is a cosmic quality to every moral struggle. You win or lose for more than yourself. The eleventh chapter of Hebrews tells about the invisible witnesses ever surrounding the Christian, the saints of faith—Abraham, Moses, Enoch, an innumerable company. And Chapter 12 begins with: "Wherefore seeing we also are compassed about with so great a cloud of witnesses, let us lay aside every weight, and the sin which doth so easily beset us, and let us run with patience the race that is set before us, looking unto Jesus the author and finisher of our faith." The picture is of a Roman race track. High up in the colosseum on all sides are those who have fought their good fight for character and won the battle, and they're looking down on you, and trusting you'll run your little race of life like a man—yes, run it even better than they did. And, Christian, you never enter into temptation without such invisible companions, the heavenly colosseum. They are faithful, they stand by.

Isn't it true that most of us conquer temptation because we don't dare let someone else down, someone who we know in our heart of hearts is in the struggle with us? We all have our invisible witnesses, our own saints—a father, a teacher, a son. We are all spiritually part of those we love. And the fact that they're there makes all the difference in the world, as does the fact that God is there, and Jesus our Lord and Savior, those who have loved us

and prayed for us and mystically stand by in our most desperate
moments of choice.

> I would be true [Why?] for there are those who trust me
> I would be pure for there are those who care.

Yes, remember in your temptation you are never alone. God is
faithful, God stands by. Others do too. They are witness to your
race.

So when you are tempted, Paul suggests, don't treat yourself as
an exception. And remember that you are never alone. But Paul
goes on: "God will with the temptation also make a way to
escape." By escape he doesn't mean an easy way out, he means that
in every moral trial God gives us an alternative. What Paul is saying is that every temptation to evil in this life is also a temptation
to some sort of good, if we only realize it. Have you ever thought
of that? Too often we think of temptation as one-sided, always
temptation to evil. But every moral crisis is double: it really offers
two choices, not one. It always presents an alternative to evil. It
always has God's way of escape. See if that isn't so; every temptation to evil you'll have in this world is actually also a temptation
to some sort of good.

This is why the Christian Church has always been willing to
admit that in some ways temptation is a good thing. A person who
is never tempted is simply morally anemic. He may not do any
harm in life, but the trouble is he won't do much good either. So,
are you tempted to lust? Then remember you are being tempted
that very moment to choose the highest type of love. Are you
tempted to be dishonest? Remember at the same moment you are
being tempted to find integrity of character. Are you tempted to
anger? You're also being tempted to a self-control. Are you
tempted to doubt God? The very temptation to doubt is also a
temptation to a deeper faith. You see, there are two paths out of
every temptation experience—the luring path of evil, but the
equally luring path of good.

This, I'm convinced, is the secret of victorious Christian living.
You can go through life always regarding temptation as something
negative, to flee from and fear. If you do, I'll guarantee you'll lose

every time; as the Negro spiritual has it, "the devil will get you in the end." But there's another way to look at temptation, and Paul knew it, and that is to realize that in the long run the most tempting things, the most alluring things, are the good things; they have the final fascination. And you and I will never be morally victorious until we know and believe that. Some of you have doubtless heard of Dwight L. Moody. He built the Northfield Schools from the money received in his great evangelistic campaigns. There on a certain hill, which has become sacred to many of us in summer conferences, they say he once wanted to build a chapel. With his typical humor, what do you think he called the place? "Temptation Hill." "For," said Moody, "some day, someone just won't be able to resist building a church there." And this minute high on Temptation Hill stands one of New England's loveliest chapels.

Don't forget God's alternative, the temptation to good in every temptation to evil. Enter your moral battles with joy, unafraid, and on every Temptation Hill of your life you'll raise a chapel to the glory of your God.

III.

SPECIFICALLY TO THE YOUNG

FIFTEEN

Falling in Love Outside Your Faith

MY SUBJECT is a difficult one: "Falling in Love Outside Your Faith." For students this is largely a problem of Protestants falling in love with Catholics and Catholics falling in love with Protestants; love affairs with those who share the great faith of Judaism are infrequent among us and certainly less complicated. But for many of us the Protestant-Catholic issue is both frequent and complicated, either here or at home, and there is no easy solution. As a minister of the Church of Christ, my task is to be both practical and honest with you.

I should say right off that I'm a great believer in young love. Being a college chaplain and living on the campus I have to be. And we all like to think that being in love is the best of all possible situations. I believe it is, if it's realistic and faces facts. I'm proud, as you are, that here in America people of different faiths associate freely. Where we associate freely it's natural that we fall in love. You know how it goes. Here's a fine fellow, we'll call him John. His folks are good Presbyterians and come originally from bonnie Scotland. Here's the young lady, Mary. Her folks are from County Cork, good old Irish, attend St. Agnes' Church. Both have gone to the public schools, both come to college. And here they get to know each other. They pretend to study together in the library, they light each other's cigarettes on the quad, they walk together under the stars or in the full brightness of the moon, they kiss good night at the entrance to the women's dormitory. They go steady; they get pinned; nearing graduation they think of getting married. It makes sense all round. And then they face it, what perhaps out of plain decency they have avoided talking about: the matter of religion. Hard facts have to be faced. Mary goes to her priest; he's kind and understanding as most priests are, but very insistent. John comes to me, let's say. What do I advise?

Of course, what anyone says varies with the individual, but by and large, certain things should be made clear when a Protestant falls in love with a Catholic. My first piece of advice is: *count on a long engagement; go slow.* Statistically there's more than twice as much chance that your marriage will go on the rocks than if you married someone of your own faith. The Maryland Report of 12,000 young people made by the American Council on Education came to the following percentages: where both parents were Protestant 6.8 per cent of the homes were broken; where both parents were Roman Catholic 6.4 per cent were broken; in the case of mixed marriages the percentage was 15.2 per cent, considerably over twice as much. Now to be fair, we should remember that statistics may not tell the story of your love; they're not an infallible guide to personality. And we should point out that the Maryland Report goes on to say that where there was no religion the percentage of broken homes was even higher, 16.7 per cent: I wish a lot of Protestant parents would remember that. They get excited over their son or daughter's going with a Catholic, but so far as I can see, it doesn't faze them one bit should they find the boy friend or girl friend to be a charming but complete pagan. Be that as it may, statistics are a warning, a warning to go slow, to look before you leap.

My second suggestion is that both of you together *study the Roman Catholic and Protestant positions on marriage and discuss them openly and frankly.* Mind you, I think both should read these statements on marriage together if possible, so that you not only read words but get each other's immediate and instinctive reaction. That first and instinctive reaction may be all-important for the future of your love; don't try to avoid it but face it honestly.

The Roman Catholic dogma on this matter of mixed marriages is very plain. It is summed up in the Code of Canon Law which no priest, no matter how understanding, could or would change. Let me quote Pope Pius XI: "Everywhere and with the greatest strictness the Catholic Church forbids marriages between baptized persons, one of whom is a Catholic and the other a member of a schismatical or heretical sect; and if there is, added to this, the danger of the falling away of the Catholic party and the perversion of the children, such a marriage is forbidden also by the divine law." Note the official attitude toward Protestants; they are heretics, schismatics, liable to lead to the falling away of the Catholic member and the perversion of children: that's plain enough. We go on to find that marriage is a sacrament of the Church, that it can be valid only if performed by a priest. For that reason before it can be performed by the priest the Protestant must sign the following agreement: "I, the undersigned, not a member of the Catholic Church, wishing to contract marriage with Mary, a member of the Catholic Church, propose to do so with the understanding that the marriage bond thus contracted is indissoluble, except by death. I promise on my word and honor that I will not in any way hinder or obstruct the said Mary in the exercise of her religion, and that all children of either sex born of our marriage shall be baptized and educated in the Catholic faith and according to the teaching of the Catholic Church, even though the said Mary should be taken away by death. . . ." This is what is known as the Antenuptial Agreement to be signed by the Protestant. On the other side is the paper to be signed by the Catholic stating that "she will prudently work for the conversion of the non-Catholic." This secondary pledge is required by Canon 1062. Again that's clear enough: the Protestant must not interfere with the faith of the Catholic but the Catholic must prudently work for the conversion of the Protestant and the children must be reared as Catholics.

Now to many Protestants these stipulations are simply unfair and out of the question. Protestants believe, as do Catholics, that marriage is a sacrament and to be celebrated in the Church.

But they do not believe that the priests of the Catholic Church have exclusive authority over true marriages, nor that people should bind their consciences by any such agreement, or mortgage the possibility of growth together in such sacred matters as the religion of children or the conversion to another faith. May I add that to some Catholics this also seems false and extreme. That's why I say: read the laws together and talk them over. How much does the Catholic really believe them? How much is the Protestant revolted? How strong are you in your own faith and, perhaps more important, how understanding are you of the faith of the other person? These are the all-important questionss to ask and answer. Don't try to avoid them.

My third piece of advice is: *as young people have the greatest sympathy and patience with your two sets of parents and relatives*. Remember the two of you are in love. That covers a lot of tension or misunderstanding: you know each other and you trust each other. But your poor parents are not in such a happy frame of mind. Both the Catholic parents and the Protestant are worried about the social consequences. What will Aunt Agatha say who's head of the Presbyterian Ladies' Aid and what about Francis who's a Jesuit priest or Uncle Dave who's in the Holy Name Society? And behind this social pressure there's the plain fact that most families have traditions of religious strife, memories of harsh treatment and social insult. The Catholic thinks of puritanic Boston where the Irish were always treated as inferior to the Yankees. The Protestant thinks of Spain where even today Protestants cannot be buried in a cemetery, but only in an open field. Besides, a lot of families move in circles quite isolated from other faiths—like the deacon in my former church who came from the South and openly said: "I never even saw a Catholic until I was twenty-one years old and moved north." But that's how it goes. All I'm saying is: be patient; it's probably a lot easier for you than your parents.

My next word is in the interest of tolerance. If you want a happy marriage together, *the two of you, both Protestant and Catholic, will have to bend over backwards in mutual respect and understanding,* and deliberately and intelligently set up such a program. Whether you like it or not, you are not going to be able to stay the same sort of Catholic you were before you fell in love with a Protestant, nor the same sort of Protestant before you fell in love with a Catholic. If you're honest with each other, you're going to change a bit in religion because of this experience of love. The Catholic member simply can't believe that his Protestant wife or husband is a potential "perverter of children's faith" as the dogma would state. Nor can the Protestant look upon his partner's faith as sheer mumbo jumbo and superstition. At its best a mixed marriage is always an experiment in understanding. And you always have to set up such an experiment deliberately.

This means you'll count on certain practical routines. Before marriage you will have at least six weeks' instruction in each other's faith. The Catholic church requires this of the Protestant member; as a Protestant minister I require it of the Catholic. The priest says: "This is not to convert you; it's so that you will understand the faith of your partner." I say the same words to the Catholic. And after marriage the process must go on. As a Catholic you should go with your wife or husband to the Protestant church at least a couple of times a year. And as a Protestant you should go to midnight mass on Christmas Eve, when the candles glimmer and the music is at its loveliest and the Catholic world welcomes the birth of our Lord with a reverence and a holy mystery we Protestants seldom achieve. In other words, statistics are against you, so bend over backwards to make your love not an example of religious indifference but a true tolerance. And true tolerance can be bought only at the price of daily tokens of understanding and respect.

Finally—and this is the hardest thing I have to say, but I think it's psychologically sound—*make your decision about the faith of your children before you come to the marriage altar*. If you are married in a Catholic Church, naturally you promise that your children will be brought up in that faith. If you are married by a Protestant minister, though you will never have to sign a paper nor coerce your conscience, the understanding should be that yours will be a Protestant family. In other words, don't delay this major decision until later on when it may become a great source of friction and distrust. Or don't try any silly compromise: the boys will be Catholics and the girls Protestants. Or don't fool yourself that you'll let the children grow up without any church and then decide for themselves: such an arrangement usually means your children grow up pagans. No, no matter how hard it is, decide before you're married and let the form of your ceremony, Protestant or Catholic, symbolize publicly your decision. Only in this way will your marriage have any possible peace of mind.

Remember, this decision is not always made one way. There are as many mixed marriages performed in Protestant churches as in Catholic. As a matter of fact, there may be more, and for very good reasons. In Protestant churches there is an atmosphere of tolerance and understanding that often gives a young couple of mixed background in faith an entirely new sense of freedom. No one church claims to be the only true one. No priest or minister interferes in the intimate details of your family life, in such matters as birth control, the schools your children may attend, or the decisions of life-and-death your family doctor may be called upon to make at a hospital. No one teaches your children that there is only one Christian truth and that their parents are heretics if they don't believe it. In Protestant families you can discuss religion freely, without the embarrassment of a paper you have had to sign, a paper forcing one of you to engage in conversion activities and forcing the other to keep silent. In Protestant churches you can find a wealth of variety of forms of worship and habits of prayer, so that over the years the two of you may hope to discover a church in which you can feel at home and which both of you and your children can attend together. In other words, your Christian faith can be a growing thing, not imposed by outside authority. The two of you can grow together, without the sinking feeling that one of you had to give up his faith for the sake of love. These are some of the reasons why, when the decision has to be made, many couples choose the Protestant way rather than the Roman Catholic.

Even so, it is not an easy way for any young person to take and I would not wish the pain of such a decision upon anyone. But if two people take each other's religion seriously, and after soul-searching come to a serious and mutual understanding, then God bless them. Such complete honesty at the deepest level of life ought certainly to put their love on the firmest ground possible.

I am told that sometimes in the Jewish wedding ceremony the rabbi presents to every couple two cups of wine. The first is the cup of joy; "drink together," he says, "of the many mutual joys that life will bring you." The other is the cup of sorrow. It is a little heavier and the wine is very bitter, but no marriage is complete without it. Far earlier than most, young people of different faiths must learn to drink that second cup together. And perhaps better than we know, their love is joined in the mutual tasting of some sorrow.

SIXTEEN

To the Campus Romeo

MY SUBJECT is "What Christianity Has to Say to the Campus Romeo." The campus Romeo is a student who "plays the field" in matters of love. There's nothing wrong with that; it may be a good idea at college. But the campus Romeo usually makes love a game. His goal is a certain number of sexual conquests. He often descends on the younger women on campus. Perhaps I shouldn't call him a Romeo: a Romeo might be thought of as standing at the foot of a balcony and strumming a guitar. This fellow is not interested in balconies or guitars. Perhaps a Don Juan would be a better name, or a wolf, or what have you.

Now I don't want you to have the impression that college campuses are full of such people. Indeed, I'm quite impressed with the sensible way most college men and women conduct themselves on this matter of sexual relations, generally speaking. As students your behavior is more conventional than your talk. Indeed, even those of you who get a bad reputation in sexual relationships are usually better than your reputation: the recent Jacob Report on "Changing Values in College" has shown this. But there is a good deal of confusion, particularly about the Christian understanding of sex. Promiscuity, for instance, is not endorsed, but neither is purity or chastity considered too essential. As one student writes: "I want a morality with elbow room." Well, that's the issue: how much freedom, how much elbow room? How far do you go, or don't?

Now biology has lots to say about sex, and surely psychology, but the Christian religion has something to say, too, therefore, in this sermon. The apostle Paul in his Epistle to the Romans writes: "I beseech you therefore, brethren, by the mercies of God, that ye present your bodies a living sacrifice, holy, acceptable unto God" (Rom. 12:1). Your bodies, mind you, are his concern, not your souls, or your spirits, or your intellects. In another letter: "Know ye not that your body is the temple of the Holy Spirit?" (I Cor. 6:19). For a Jew the temple was the center of his worship; Paul speaks of the body as being something just as holy. He goes on to say: "Therefore glorify God in your body." The men and women of Corinth who first read those words knew exactly what Paul was talking about. They were living in a wide-open town. High on the hill stood the temple of Aphrodite with its thousand sacred prostitutes. In their religion those people were worshiping their goddess with their bodies. But your bodies, says Paul to the Christians, are temples also, but of the Holy Spirit, and you too, in a Christian way, must glorify your God in your bodies.

Now what is the Christian understanding of sex? What do we mean: glorify God in our bodies? What does our faith have to say to the campus Romeo, or the Romeo in us all?

Right off, we should realize what the Christian understanding of sex is *not. It is not hedonism,* for one thing. Hedonism is the idea that sex is justified for immediate pleasure and lets it go at that. "Eat, drink, and be merry for tomorrow you die." Sex is part of the merriment of life. Quite obviously, Christianity does not fit in with this sort of thinking. We are never children of the moment in sex or anything else; we never eat, drink, or are merry with a careless conscience. The Romeo who pursues pleasure for its own sake and adds pleasure to pleasure sooner or later ends up bored. This is the hedonistic paradox: the person who pursues pleasure never really finds it; pleasure is a by-product, never the goal of life. Hedonism as such is out.

Nor again is the Christian understanding of sex to be equated with *prudery or Victorianism*. The Victorian was afraid of the body; it was evil, it was embarrassing. At the turn of the century it was considered good taste in Boston to keep books by male and female authors on separate library shelves. And a lot of churches are still Victorian, no doubt about that. Kinsey has found that the more religious people are the less frequent are their sexual practices and relations. Well, this may be so, but it is not the Christian faith as such. The body is God's creation. It is good. As T. S. Eliot puts it in "The Rock":

> Visible and invisible, two worlds meet in Man;
> Visible and invisible must meet in His Temple;
> You must not deny the body.[1]

Nor again is the Christian understanding of sex to be equated with a *biologic outlet*. Kinsey has defined sex as a "normal biologic function acceptable in whatever form it is manifested." For the purposes of his study that definition is adequate. For the Christian it is inadequate, as I believe Kinsey himself admitted. Sex for the Christian is more than a biologic function or outlet. Man is more than a mammal, and in every sexual act more than biology is involved; the total person is involved. Culture is as much a part of sex, and morals, and psychology, and religion, as biology itself. The Christian can simply never allow himself to be misled by any partial or fragmentary definition of the nature of man, helpful as that definition may be for a particular scientific experiment. Sex is not simply a biologic function.

So much, then, for what the Christian understanding of sex is not—not hedonism, nor Victorianism, nor biologic outlet. But let's go on to the more positive. What of a positive nature has Christianity to say to the campus Romeo, or the sexual life of any one of us?

First of all, *The Christian faith teaches us to look at our sexual lives sacramentally*. What do I mean? A sacrament is a mystery, the mystery of the union of physical and spiritual; one cannot be separated from the other. So, for the Christian, sex is always the physical accompaniment of a spiritual union, and in it you are

[1] *Collected Poems of T. S. Eliot* (New York: Harcourt, Brace, 1936).

always faced with the deep mystery of that union. This is the sacramental understanding of sex in which the Church has always believed.

You see, Christianity is not actually a spiritual religion. In many ways it seems materialistic because it never separates the physical from the spiritual. The very word for soul in the Hebrew Bible, *nephesh,* means a union of body and spirit. So also in the New Testament we have the Greek *pneuma.* Perhaps this sacramental view can best be expressed in modern literature. Some of you have read Alan Paton's great novel, *Too Late the Phalarope.*[2] Pieter, a young Afrikaner, is speaking. His wife, a strict Protestant, is unable to love him in a completely physical way because she feels that she should be spiritual, and that the body is a necessary evil. He speaks to her: "It's all together, the body and mind and soul, between a man and a woman. When you love me as you've done, I'm comforted in them all. And when I love you as I've done, it's you I love, your body and mind and soul." And later on, speaking to himself, he says: "And I wanted to cry out at her that I could not put the body apart from the soul, and that the comfort of her body was more than a thing of the flesh, but was also a comfort of the soul, and why it was, I could not say, and why it should be, I could not say, but there was in it nothing that was ugly or evil, but only good." That's the Bible speaking in modern prose. It's the Christian way of looking at life sacramentally.

Because of this sacramental view of sex, the Christian Church recommends to its young people chastity before marriage. Not that anyone is ruined otherwise—not at all. The Christian faith is no cheap legalism; it has no set of laws fixed and final; it's a morality with more elbow room than most of us imagine. But because of its sacramental view of life, it knows that sex relationships have effects on people even when they are not intended. The physical always does something to the spiritual. You never go scot free from a sex experience. Romeo may think he can "love them and

[2] New York: Scribner's, 1953. This quotation and some of the argument that follows are from William Hamilton, *The Christian Man* (Philadelphia: Westminster Press, 1956).

leave them," he may even laugh it off, "Boy, what a night"—but he's a man who's broken a symbol, a symbol that "It's all together, the body and mind and soul, between a man and a woman. . . ." And you can never treat that symbol casually without becoming yourself a casual person, who can never be total in any human relationship, can never be wholehearted or complete. So, for a Christian all physical acts have a built-in meaning; they are never just physical. Shaking hands means one thing; holding hands means another; kissing still another. And to carry the physical act beyond its built-in meaning is ultimately self-destructive. For the Christian the sexual act is a symbol of love "till death us do part." That's its meaning.

First of all, then, Christian faith says: learn to look at your sexual life sacramentally. Secondly, it says, *try to emphasize in every way possible the humanness of sex, the profoundly personal.* We live in an age that dehumanizes sex, takes it apart from the person. Indeed, often you cannot even think sexually these days in terms of the whole body of a person. In the movies sex is the bust of Marilyn Monroe, or the legs of Jane Russell, or the walk of some other piece of feminine beauty. You can't even see a body as a body any more; it's always some part of a body. And if you dehumanize that much in the realm of the body, only see a piece of it, then how easy it is to leave out all the other sides of personality, until sex is "a thing you do, not a person you meet."

I remember one sentence in William Gibson's little book, later made into a movie, called *Cobweb.* Dr. McIver says: "I'm not talking about sex; I'm talking about people. Sex is communication; it requires adults." And that's a good way to look at it. Sexual relations involve the most intimate and personal kind of knowledge you and I can ever have of another person on this earth. In such relations a man knows what it is to be a man and helps his partner to know what it is to be truly a woman. So, don't dehumanize the most truly personal relationship of this earth. Sex is communication; it requires adults, grown-up people.

Here the promiscuous man, the campus Romeo, makes his mistake. He never is quite able to see another person as a real person. He always sees that person as something of an object. The girl may be an object to satisfy his sexual tensions. The girl may be an object to comfort his ego: "Prove that you love me," he says. Or sex may be a way in which he takes out his frustrations on others. Thwarted in his own personality he finds in sex his only sense of power: at least he can feel important in this. Or else sex is a way in which he escapes from life, evades its tensions and issues. Talk to any promiscuous student and you will find two things: sex is either an attempt to affirm a frustrated self or else a way to get away from an overstimulated self. In any case, the partner is an object, and such a relationship slowly dehumanizes both the man and the woman.

For the Christian this is the only way in which sex can be said to be sin. Sin is never sensuality as such; sin is self-love. But nowhere does self-love reveal itself more openly than in sensual acts. Mind you, the body is never the cause of sin, but the body may be the stage with the curtain up, the theater, in which self-love best preens and parades itself.

Two things, then, the Christian faith says: learn to look at your sexual life sacramentally. Do everything you can to emphasize the humanness of sex, the profoundly personal, seeing sex not as a thing you do but as a person you meet. Then this is third: if we are to be Christian in our sexual relationships, if we are to glorify God in our bodies, then *we must be socially responsible.* Sex is our link to the past and our link to the future, and no Christian can enter into it without a deep and lasting sense of the sheer wonder of ongoing life. After all, our years on this earth are few enough, a mere "moment between sun and frost" as the poet has it. But we are also part of an endless chain of life, and we are responsible to God and to mankind to see that that chain does not break at our link, nor life be wasted because of our indifference or selfishness or lack of faith. In the mystery of sex is hidden the mystery of new life, ongoing life, and only the most shallow soul can be careless before that mystery.

This truth, I know, is supremely important to most of you. Before me are some whose fathers and mothers once sat in this very chapel and worshiped God and loved each other and tried to communicate that love to the future in you people. It matters very little that they "made love" differently from the way you do. What is important is the continuity of the generations that surrounds every act of love. It's not something two people do together in some dark corner. Sex is never private; it's always public in its effects and its responsibilities. It forms the family, and in the family not only do you reproduce yourself physically but all the attitudes you bring to your sexual life are strangely continued and either bless or damn those who come after you. The Jacob Report on college students states that seven out of ten of you expect your future family to provide you more satisfaction in this life than any other activity. If it's so important, if this is going to be the center of happiness for all your mortal days, then it calls for only the best you have to give to it.

So don't be a campus Romeo, then live to regret it. The Christian ethic for sex is a difficult one, but it may be worth a good try. Recently I read an anecdote about O. Henry, the American story writer, whose real name was Sydney Porter. As a young man Porter was put in prison for embezzlement. He met a guard there named Oren Henry, and when the time came for Porter to leave the prison, rather than carry out his old name, which had been disgraced, he took the name of his guard, O. Henry, out into public life and wrote under it. And the story is that, as he went through the prison doors, the old guard waved to him and said: "Take good care of our name."

I think there are generations, older and younger, saying that to you during these days when love is so crucial. In your intimate lives take good care of the good name that others have given you. I beseech you, glorify God in your bodies.

SEVENTEEN

God and Your Car

I AM going to talk with you about God and your car. Perhaps the subject occurred to me because, like many other Americans these days, I have been looking over the new models of automobiles and listening to all the wonders of their horsepower, their speed, their beauty, and their new gadgets. Or perhaps it's because this is the holiday season, Christmas following Thanksgiving and New Year's Christmas, a season when we are all aware of the menace as well as the beauty of our automobiles. Over this season several hundred of us will lose our lives in accidents. Last year about 36,000 died in this way and this year may be comparable. That figure alone is larger than the number of deaths of our soldiers in Korea. Yes, a constant source of joy, the automobile is also a constant source of sorrow and heartache, particularly at this holiday season. Or perhaps the subject occurred to me because of an article I read a while ago. After giving all the statistics of safety, it ended with the statement that the basic problem in the slaughter of the American road is an inward and a spiritual one. It's that of "a man driving a machine that is running wild because it lacks a spiritual governor."[1] The author of

[1] See "Save That Man's Life," *The Christian Century*, January 12, 1955, for this quotation and statistics in this sermon.

the article called on the churches to do something about it. There's nothing wrong with the cars, you see; it's the people who are at fault. And what's wrong with the people? Ultimately something inward, something spiritual. Our machines run wild in this world when they lack a spiritual governor.

Let's think then for a few minutes about God and your car. What has religion to say about the way you drive? The Christian Church talks frequently about the horror of war; does it have anything to say about the equal horror of accidents?

Perhaps we can start where Jesus started, with what we call the Great Commandments of Mark 12:30–31. You know them: "Thou shalt love the Lord thy God with all thy heart, and soul, and mind, and strength, and thy neighbor as thyself." In other words, the goal of the Christian life is a God-inspired love which treats your neighbor with all the respect due a child of God. It's as simple as that, and yet as demanding. "Thou shalt love the Lord thy God"—that's first, But then comes an inevitable corollary of that love, an inescapable derivative: "Thou shalt love thy neighbor as thyself."

What happens when we take this twofold love of God and neighbor seriously and apply it to the way we drive? First of all, we realize as Christians that *life is a gift of God and must always be held in reverence.* That reverence does not diminish as the horsepower increases; indeed, it is all the more necessary. Albert Schweitzer, you remember, once sat in a barge going up the Ogowe River, trying to figure out what was the ultimate requirement of an ethical man, what was absolute, what you could not get behind or beyond. He wrote down several requirements on individual slips of paper: a good man is pure, is temperate, is loyal, etc. Slowly, as he thought of his own life and others, he dropped each of the slips one by one into the stream swirling behind him. Then there flashed upon his mind the phrase "Reverence for Life" and "the iron door had yielded; the path in the thicket had become visible." This seemed to Schweitzer the one absolute for a good man, the one thing you couldn't escape or get beyond.

We might add, however, that Schweitzer goes on to say that our Western civilization is dying simply because it has lost this reverence for life. You and I can certainly add plenty of footnotes to that. Perhaps it's because of the war, but we live in an age that is apt to consider life cheap. We live in an age that will be remembered in history as the age of Buchenwald and Dachau and brainwashing and a thousand scientific and efficient ways of humiliating and destroying the human. We live in an age of the new barbarian. At the end of a big-league baseball game one summer day I stopped with a friend on the ramps of the stadium. Below us thousands of people milled about. As we watched we overheard a chap wearing a college sweater saying: "Boy, I'd like to have a machine gun here and mow them all down." There he was, the new barbarian. Yes, this is an age in which we are all tempted to treat human life cheaply and our driving follows the spirit of the age. It is well, then, for the Christian to remember that life is the gift of God and the good man always reverences it wherever he finds it. God has something to say about the way you and I drive.

But not only does Christianity remind us of reverence for life; it also warns us that *power changes persons.* Thus our worst sins may come out from behind the steering wheel. The strange thing about sin is that a man may be a perfectly good man as an individual in a face-to-face situation, but give that man power, place him in a situation which is impersonal, and all his irresponsibilities and lower greed and self-centeredness will assert themselves. This is what Reinhold Niebuhr is talking about when he speaks of "moral man in immoral society." It's a real insight: a good man in a position of power often changes his ethics; he's quite different as the boss from what he is as the neighbor. So the automobile driver, a perfectly good man, with 250 horsepower in his control may be a devil. Lord Acton said: "Power corrupts and absolute power corrupts absolutely." And the most absolute sense of power some of us have comes when we are driving. For that reason, as the Christian sees it, we are most prone to sin.

Notice, then, the next time you are driving how your personality tends to change. Ordinarily you might be quite an easygoing person, but get behind that wheel and you become hostile to everybody else—"No one's going to shove me around." Ordinarily you might be quite considerate, but get behind the wheel and you become the most competitive person on the road—"Nobody's going to get ahead of me when the light turns green." Ordinarily you might be quite relaxed, but behind the wheel you strain every muscle to make time and get some place fast for no reason at all except to get there. Or notice how, if someone gets ahead of you, all your unconscious prejudices come out quite irrationally. You call people names that you would never want repeated. But there it is. Take an honest look at yourself as a driver. The Christian faith says that the most moral man can become quite immoral when placed in a situation of power. Power changes persons; that's one aspect of sin.

There's a third aspect of Christ's Great Commandments: it is law-abidingness. Remember that Christian love is nothing sentimental; it's very much down to earth. Jesus said: "Thou shalt love thy neighbor as thyself." Often we think that means we should have an emotional reaction to human beings. We think religion is just loving everybody, a kind of blowing kisses to the world. But that's far from Jesus, very far. For him Christian love was more responsible good will than emotional ecstasy. And in terms of your automobile this means simply, first of all, law-abidingness, then courtesy, then self-control. Nothing sweet or sentimental. Christian love is always down to earth.

Let's spell it out then. *Christian love means law-abidingness.* One-third of all traffic deaths are caused by speed, by breaking the law in most cases. This, whether we like it or not, for the Christian is sin. Justice has been defined as "love at a distance." In other words, the chief way in which Christian love can ever express itself in our complicated society is through justice, through law. This is why the Christian from earliest history has been law-abiding. How easily those early disciples could have been anarchists, turned against the Roman government that was persecuting them in arena and colosseum! But, no, the apostle Paul said: "Let every soul be subject unto the higher powers. For . . . the powers that be are ordained of God. . . . For rulers are not a terror to good works, but to the evil. . . . Wherefore . . . be subject, not only for wrath, but also for conscience sake" (Rom. 13:1–5). Remember, the Christian has never been sentimental about this law of love of neighbor. Justice is "Christian love at a distance."

And Christian love means courtesy, too. Courtesy has been defined as "love in little things." Certainly this is one other expression of Christian love as it applies to the rules of the road. More than 16 per cent of all accidents are due to lack of courtesy, failure to yield the right of way, using the other fellow's side of the road instead of your own. It's really amazing how many of us behind the wheel lose all manners. What man would knock down a child or push a woman off the sidewalk in order to get ahead? In traffic a sense of manners or inward courtesy often seems to vanish. Perhaps we had better remind ourselves that in Paul's great hymn to Christian love, I Corinthians 13, one of the phrases in modern translation is "love is not rude." Another is: "Love does not insist on its rights." Christian love is expressed in courtesy.

And finally, *Christian love certainly means self-control.* Experts tell us that 30 per cent of all traffic fatalities are due to drinking,[2] but that drink as a secondary cause would make the percentage much higher. Here is not a question of whether it's right or wrong for a Christian to drink: the Church has never spoken with one voice on that. But there has been no doubt in the mind of the Christian Church that drinking, even moderate drinking, that threatens the lives of innocent people by wild driving is a sin and accountable to God himself. If love of neighbor means anything, it means that no man has the right to indulge himself at the expense of others of God's children who are just as dear to God as the man who drinks. Self-indulgence is a spiritual sin in any form, but as modern living becomes more interdependent, it becomes even more a sin. If Jesus were here today I'm sure he would say: "Thou shalt love thy neighbor by controlling thy self."

What about God and your car, then? What has religion to say to the way you drive? Simply this: The Christian is one who knows that life is the gift of God and must be held in reverence. He knows that the worst of our sins often come out behind the wheel, when power changes our personalities and makes them often in-

[2] This figure is from the National Safety Council's report for 1956, as printed in *The Christian Century,* April 9, 1958.

human. He knows that Christian love is no sentimental attachment for people but a responsible concern for others which expresses itself in law-abidingness, in courtesy, and in self-control.

They say that among the Greeks it was never the man who ran the race fastest who won it, but the man who ran the race not only fast but beautifully and true. I'm not at all sure that God expects speed out of us in this mortal life; I'm quite sure he expects us to be beautiful and true. This is the real race most of us Americans have to win these days, lest with all our sciences and skills we become a people who perish for want of a spiritual governor.

EIGHTEEN

A Sophisticated Way of Saying No
(A Sermon on College Drinking)

I NEVER knew a generation of college students that didn't like a hangout. The university may spend thousands of dollars to furnish reception rooms, but you'll pack into your cars and go over to some hole-in-the-wall. The university furnishes indirect lighting, but you'll prefer a place where the lighting is not only indirect but practically nonexistent. The university says you need plenty of space to entertain, lots of room; so off you go to a place where you practically sit on top of one another. Anyway, sometime or other, most of you will end up in the college hangout.

This brings up the question of drinking: what has Christianity to say about it? Some authorities believe that alcoholism is America's number one health and social problem—has the Church anything to contribute or suggest? Is there a Christian answer?

It may surprise you to realize right off that there isn't any one Christian answer to this matter of drinking, much as some of us might wish there were. The Bible doesn't say yes or no. The people of the Bible drank; Jesus turned water into wine at the marriage feast; Paul suggested that a little wine might be good for the stomach's sake. Drunkenness was condemned as a sin of the flesh, but there were few total abstainers. The only one I know was Samson in the Old Testament and he had so many other faults that I would hesitate to single him out. No, the Christian faith can never be reduced to any one hard and fast set of morals. Paul rightly observed, "There is liberty."

And if the Bible doesn't help, neither does church history. Baptists and Methodists are by tradition, at least since the 1830's, total abstainers; these churches went west with the frontier and their chief enemy in each town was the corner saloon. But many other denominations, plus the great European churches, believe that total abstinence is extreme and ascetic. Moderate and occasional drinking—of both laymen and clergy—is understood and allowed. Even Baptists, as they move into the upper-income brackets, tend to approve of a mild form of social drinking. So there is no hard and fast answer for all Christians, at least from history.

But all of us, I suppose, could start with the homespun wisdom of the Book of Proverbs. The author, whoever he was, gives me the impression of having "been around" town in 500 B.C. Listen to how he describes going under the influence of drink: "Look not on the wine so red that sparkles in the cup. It glides down smoothly at the first, but in the end it bites like any snake. You will be seeing odd things, you will be saying queer things. [Times haven't changed much from three thousand years ago, have they?] You will sway back and forth like a man at sea." And he concludes, "Wine is a mocker" (Prov. 20:1)—in other words, it deceives you. "Strong drink means conflict"; that's a modern translation, but one with rather accurate psychological insight. Drinking often means plenty of conflict. "None who reels under it is ever wise." I like the way he puts it. He's no ascetic, but he's no fool either. He's quite hardheaded about it all, and quite common sense. Wine *is* a mocker, strong drink is apt to mean conflict, and no one who reels under it is ever wise.

Let me be practical then today and suggest five rules for any Christian to observe as he faces the problem of drink. These apply, I believe, both to the total abstainers among us and to those who are not. My first rule is this: *Don't fall for the glamour line;*

don't be taken in by the persistent commercial build-up of drinking. The Christian man is an honest man, and, whatever drinking is, it isn't always glamorous, and we might as well call a spade a spade.

Yet, glamour is the biggest aim and advertising technique in the liquor industry, isn't it? It lives by what is called "prestige advertising." It says almost nothing about the product, but it creates associations, impressions, social concepts, which are both effective and misleading. Old Grandad stands hale and hearty before his bookcase with red-leather volumes of Shakespeare all around him and one in his hand. The impression is that if you want to be hale and hearty at eighty, and a cultured gentleman to boot, enjoy a certain whisky. The hard truth is that alcohol has little to do with making us finer students of Shakespeare. Or we read, "Cool Heads Choose Calvert's"—for men of action, wisdom, decision, achievement, and perspective. And there in front of you is the slightly worn executive type. Again, you can believe that if you want to, but the unfortunate truth is that cool heads usually choose water, and let's not be fool enough to be taken in by anything else. So it seems you can't do your part for the dear old class of '99 without a highball; you can't hunt or fish without beer; you can't enjoy Metropolitan Moments, whatever they may be, without one brand of liquor; you can't get married without another. Even churches get into the show. A few years ago one of our big-name firms had large display advertisements at Christmas of the finest cathedrals of Christendom, and below was the pious line: "Greetings at this holy season from your favorite distiller." Well, Christians, we can start by saying "hokum" to most of this. Let's not deceive ourselves. Drinking doesn't necessarily increase your virtues or bring out your better self. For many people drinking is a total tragedy—let's at least be that honest.

Rule number two: *Develop a technique of getting along with a drinking crowd without compromising your own convictions.* This is important. Too often Christian young people follow the drinking crowd because they simply don't know what else to do. They've been given no techniques, only the prohibition "don't drink," so out of pure self-consciousness at a party, fear of awkwardness or of being impolite, they fall into line. The Book of Exodus (23:2) says: "Do not follow a multitude to do evil," but believe me, it's not easy to find a smooth technique for carrying that out. In other words, unless you're lucky you can't always escape the drinking crowd, in business, in social contacts, in college, even in the churches. How then do you get along with it?

Well, there's a sophisticated way of saying "No," and every Christian young person should develop such a technique. If you find yourself at a cocktail party and someone insists on handing you a drink, don't make an issue of it; take it, set it down on a table if you don't want it, and let it go at that. You don't have to drink cocktails any more than you have to eat artichokes or Liederkranz cheese. I'm always amazed at the college man or woman who for ten years has had the backbone to refuse to eat carrots but suddenly wilts when offered a Tom Collins. At that point a man's stomach is his castle. Or you may ask your hostess if she would mind your having something else to drink. She may give you a look as if to say, "Too bad such a young man has ulcers already," but usually there's something else provided. In any case, you never have to drink: fifty million Americans don't.

Of course, there are times when even a teetotaler needs a sense of humor. I recall a fashionable wedding I conducted in Boston and the glittering reception which followed. Finally all gathered in a circle to toast the bride in champagne. All the guests were supplied except myself. There was an awful pause. Everyone wondered what had happened. Then in came the butler with a tea wagon, a huge silver bowl with ice in it, and on top two tiny five-cent bottles of ginger ale, which he proceeded to open with great ceremony. I got one; the trouble was, the other one went to a ninety-year-old lady in a wheelchair! Well, so it goes. *De gustibus non est disputandum.* Remember, there's a sophisticated way of saying "No."

Rule number three: *Don't ever think you've got more control than other people.* This is the mistake we "intellectuals" often make. We somehow think that, because we have highly trained brains, we can more easily escape the mechanical reactions of our bodies. We know how far we can go; we know when we can take it and leave it alone. All I can say is that Pascal, one of the geniuses of all time, once wrote of human nature: "Never forget, we are as much automatic as intellectual."

As a matter of fact, the more intelligent a person is, the more hopeless drinker he can become. Talking with one of the leaders of Alcoholics Anonymous recently I asked what success the movement had had in drying up alcoholics. He said that about 50 per cent of the people who joined their groups could be cured within a short time; 25 per cent might lapse now and again, but in a longer period be cured. "What about the other 25 per cent," I asked, "the incurables?" His answer was, "Most of them are the intellectuals. They simply won't admit there's anything wrong with them. They still think they can control themselves. They don't know how helpless they really are." I need not push that point farther. Never forget, as human beings we are as much automatic as intellectual. Don't think you're anything exceptional, that you have more control than other people.

Then, in the fourth place, if a Christian would keep his soul in an increasingly alcoholic society, *he's got to watch his own tendencies to escape from reality.* For isn't it apparent that men drink, not for a physical pleasure primarily, but for a psychological release? Drinking is too often an easy way out of responsibility, to live without reason or judgment, to forget disappointments and frustrations, to release tensions. The Book of Proverbs is right: "Strong drink means conflict." Yes, it means conflict too easily resolved, and falsely, oh, how falsely, escaped.

This, of course, is where the occasional drinker always has to be honest and careful with himself. The psychological tendency to escape responsibility which comes even with light drinking is often as much a menace to others as the stupor which comes with heavy drinking. The National Safety Council says this about driving: "One-third of all fatalities on the road may be caused by liquor." Why? Because the driver was drunk? Not at all. Drunken men seldom attempt to drive. It's the moderate drinker who causes the accidents. But again, why? Not because he can't hear or see or control the car, but because with a few drinks in him he's much too overconfident. He takes chances he would never take when sober.

He has the attitude, "I don't care." And it's this I-don't-care attitude which menaces himself and others—this easy escape from the demands of reality. And this disease, of which drinking is only a symptom, is always sin to the Christian. Ultimately, there can be no reconciliation between "the fellowship of the concerned," which is the Church, and "the fellowship of the unconcerned," which, alas, all too often is the philosophy of men and women when they drink. That's why I would say particularly to college men and women: drinking may only be one sign of a tendency to escape difficulty and responsibility. Watch it.

How then should a Christian face the problem of drink? First, strip it of its glamour. Second, develop a technique of getting along with the drinking crowd without losing your convictions. Third, don't overestimate your control. Fourth, watch those tendencies we all have to escape from reality. *Finally, I'd remind us as Christians never to neglect the spiritual center of life,* that sense of supreme purpose, destiny, and duty to God which saves us all from that "cosmic loneliness" which we know is at the heart of many a chronic drinker, and many a sick soul. Drinking is partly a sickness, but it may also be a sin, an alienation, a separation from the Eternal. For without an ultimate purpose in life, men give themselves to lesser purposes; without a God to worship they usually worship themselves, and themselves at their worst.

The final answer is a deep religious faith. If America is becoming increasingly addicted to drink it's because there's a terrible emptiness at her heart. It used to be that when New England villages were first built, a custom called "centering the town" was followed. The boundaries of the village were determined, the lines drawn from the four corners to the middle. Where the lines crossed the town was to be "centered." And there at the exact center the early Americans built a church to the glory of God.

Yes, "wine is a mocker and no one who reels under it is ever wise." But it's also a terrible revealer, a revealer of the emptiness of much of our living. We have a civilization, I'm afraid, that no longer is centered in God.

NINETEEN

The Christian Soldier
(A Sermon on Military Service)

IN THE clear morning air of July 31, 1944, a lone French reconnaissance plane flew out from the shore of Africa and headed across the blue Mediterranean for the enemy-held land of Italy. There was one occupant of the plane, one of the most talented young French authors of modern times. His name was Antoine de Saint-Exupéry. Some of you know him from his books, *Wind, Sand and Stars* and *The Little Prince*. He was a man of great culture, a lover of humanity and a Christian. He never returned from his mission, for that evening in Italy a young German pilot wrote down a perfunctory entry in his report: "One enemy reconnaissance plane brought down in flames over the sea." Two years later, when peace came, this young German officer was being questioned by the Allied victors. He, too, was a man of considerable culture, a lover of humanity and a Christian. He had a fine library, and the captain who was interviewing him happened to ask whom he considered the most promising author of the twentieth century. The German's answer was immediate: "A young Frenchman. His name is Antoine de Saint-Exupéry."

I tell that story because it puts in dramatic fashion the tragedy of any Christian in war. If as individuals these two could have met, they would have been close friends. If as Christians they could have known each other, they would have had much in common. But in a world of war no such choice is ever given. You meet, but you meet to kill each other. And here is the tragedy: you never kill another human being without killing something of yourself.

The tragedy of war, this personal dilemma, perhaps doesn't mean too much to you students right off. It's not that you're lighthearted or naive; as a matter of fact, you worry about war quite a bit. When the Suez crisis was at its height you stayed by your radios. You made wisecracks about the airline posters in the Union, "See you in Cairo," but that was a sort of defense you put up. You didn't really want to get messed up in it, you didn't want to see anyone in Cairo. No, you're intelligent enough to know that war is no picnic. It's countless bodies lying in the streets of Budapest covered with lime—a clean and a quick way to get rid of them. It's mammoth destruction—what has taken centuries to build, gone in a moment. It's death by radiation, either quick or slow. It's politicians signing papers and then wondering who won. But it is not enough to know war intellectually; you've got to feel it within. War is a slow yellow cloud that sinks over the mind so that after a while you don't know truth from falsehood. It's hatred sanctified. It's doing things you never dreamed your hands could do, seeing things you never dreamed your eyes would see. It's being so familiar with death you almost forget what life, real life, is all about. It's being bored, bored, endlessly bored, with just surviving. In other words, you're lucky if you come out with your body all in one piece, but you're luckier if you come out with your soul. That's why every Christian prays for peace. That's why like Jesus in Gethsemane he says: "If it be possible, let this cup pass from me." I hope you never go to war. I hope our country never again goes to war.

But if war does come, and as has been obvious from the last few months, quite easily and realistically it may, even if it is just limited war, then what does the Christian do? *Historically there are three courses open to the Christian, three choices.* He may refuse to fight, be a conscientious objector, a pacifist: from the days of the Roman Empire this has been one logical choice for a Christian. Or he may declare that this is a holy war for God and the Church. At times, Roman Catholicism in its struggle against Communism—and even some Protestants—have come close to this position. The obvious historical precedent is the Crusades. A war may be for a Christian a holy war, a crusade. Or, and here the vast majority of us no doubt stand, he may declare as did St. Augustine that this is a "just and mournful war." In other words, we are under no illusions that Christianity will be advanced by dropping atomic bombs and turning millions of God's children into cinders: it's a dirty mess, war is, nothing holy about it. It's a mournful thing, a tragic thing. But it may be the best we can do, the best relative justice we can achieve—a just but mournful war. These are essentially the three choices open to any Christian—to be a pacifist, or a Crusader, or a penitent participant.

Notice two things. First of all, *there is no one Christian choice,* no one pure and perfect choice when war comes. Sometimes the pacifist thinks he is the only one making a Christian choice, the only pure one. After all, he's doing no one any harm. Or, as a distinguished rabbi said at the beginning of the last war: "At least I'll keep my conscience clean." But does he? Not really. When your country is at war, your very neutrality is the enemy's greatest comfort and you might as well be realistic about it. You're not clean, you're just letting other men do your dirty work. There's a fastidiousness about a pacifist and, unless he's careful, a big bit of self-righteousness: "I'm the only Christian on the block." And the Crusader with his holy war is certainly not pure. He makes strange allies in his godly war and in the name of God usually does things that make millions curse his God and die. The most terrible things imaginable are often done by men who believe *Gott Mit Uns.* And the third choice, that of Augustine, admits sin and evil in its very definition. A war may be just, but it is never perfectly just. Every choice a Christian makes in a war situation has sin and evil in it. There is obviously no one Christian choice.

But having said this, I must point out a second thing: when war comes, *there is one choice a Christian never has, and that is to drift, to be choiceless.* You see, a Christian can be a conscientious objector to war, or a Christian can be a conscientious soldier in war, but one thing he can't be—an unconscientious soldier or an unconscientious objector. He can't be a person who never faces the problems of conscience or makes any choices but just drifts with the tide. Moral indifference is never a Christian option, nor is moral insensitivity. Along the Niagara River, a mile or two above the Falls, there is the sign: "Do not drift beyond this point." Christianity says that to each of us, particularly those of us of college age. Up to this point you may have drifted, let life, or the gang, or your parents, make all the decisions for you. But you're adults now, and beyond this point you had better not drift, you had better choose. If you are a soldier, be a conscientious soldier, or a pacifist, or a Crusader. "My country right or wrong" is not a quotation from the Bible. It is the drifter's creed.

So far I've been a bit abstract; let me be concrete. Most of you men in front of me will be in uniform in short order. It may be a shorter time than many of you think, particularly if the world crisis continues. You may not even finish your college career, who knows?

Now I hate war. I hate it personally. It took away one of my best college friends; he died on the beach at Anzio. It took away my only cousin, they never found him, somewhere lost on the frozen steppes of Russia. But I hate war as a Christian, too, because as a minister I've had to bury the dead, and comfort widows, and try to explain things to little children that you never can explain. For a Christian, war is a damnable thing. In many ways, I'm a pacifist. But, having said this, I must add: one of the most important things today is for you men to be Christian soldiers. The uniform never makes the man; the man makes the uniform. And here is the way I would describe a Christian man in uniform, a Christian soldier.

First of all, *he's a person who hates social injustice in whatever form he finds it.* A Christian soldier is a fighter, but he fights on big fronts, bigger than the average soldier. The average soldier fights the enemy—the Communist, the Nazi, what have you. The Christian soldier fights the enemy within the enemy, and the enemy within his own ranks, yes, even within himself. To kill off Communists and let it go at that is to suffer from occupational blindness. But to see the battle on the widest front, to hate the economic injustice and social discrimination that makes the Communist possible, is the task of the Christian soldier. He knows where the real war is and not just the battle. He's got a "big hatred" and not just a little one.

For this reason Christian soldiers know and understand each other even when they're wearing different uniforms. Abraham Lincoln was a man with a big hatred. He never forgot the slaves whipped by the masters and he vowed to avenge every drop of their blood. But Robert E. Lee, wearing quite another uniform, also had a big hatred and it was much the same as Lincoln's. For remember, after peace, one of the first Sundays in his own Episcopal church in Virginia, when a Negro woman went up to the altar to receive communion, all the white people held back, except one. General Lee went up and without hesitation received communion with her. Lee hated what Lincoln hated, social injustice to another human being. And this is what joins all Christian soldiers. They have hatreds bigger than the hatreds of war. They fight, but fight on wide fronts.

College is important in the training of a Christian soldier. Through his study of sociology, psychology, history, he sees his own society for what it is—its strengths and its weaknesses. Like a doctor he knows the difference between a symptom and a disease and fights the disease, not the symptom. He does not fall for slogans. At times he is a splendid nonconformist. So remember, men, more cowards may be born in fraternities than ever are born on battlefields. And consequently more true bravery may be shown, too, the bravery that lasts. A hatred bigger than war is always the first mark of a Christian soldier.

And this is second: *A Christian soldier is one who loves humanity, and seeks to serve humanity, even as a soldier.* Oh, I don't mean anything sentimental, like the pictures of American soldiers giving candy to the kiddies after battle—that's fine in its place and I think most Americans are bighearted people. But I mean that even in uniform a Christian should see his job as something bigger than blowing up tanks or bridges or people. A Christian is called upon to love his neighbor, and I believe that a Christian soldier, even in wartime, should see his work, shameful as it may be, as an act of love and responsibility to humanity.

You see, love is not necessarily the opposite of force; love may have to use force. It's always easy to think of Christian love expressing itself in tenderness, like a nurse who heals wounds after battle, or perhaps like the Good Samaritan in Jesus' parable. Jesus told the parable of the Good Samaritan as the highest example of Christian love of neighbor. And it's not hard to see some of our responsibilities from that: Christian love binds up wounds of men, and pours in oil, and takes the sufferer to the inn and cares for him in his pain. This compassion is what the Christian pacifist emphasizes, or the noncombatant, or the medical corps. Good Samaritanism is Christian love. But have you ever asked yourself the question: What if the Samaritan had come down that Jericho road a few minutes earlier than he did, and seen the thieves bludgeoning the traveler and wounding him and leaving him half-dead in the road? Then how might he have shown his Christian love of neighbor? Might he not have fought the thief to show love? At least that possibility cannot be overlooked. Love can be shown through the use of force, and the soldier may be as responsible to humanity as the nurse.

This is said not to condone war but to remind you that a soldier is more than a murderer, and that a Christian, when he becomes a soldier, does not escape the obligation to love God and love his neighbor. A Christian can never wear any uniform, nor can he serve any country, if he believes that that uniform or that country is enslaving, destroying, and brutalizing mankind. Your two, three, four years in the armed services are no interlude from the Christian ethic and faith. You must always answer to humanity and to God for your deeds as soldiers.

I have described the Christian soldier as one who has a hatred bigger than war, the hatred of social injustice; and as one who still feels his responsibility to love and serve mankind even through the use of force. Finally I want to emphasize that *a Christian soldier is one who all through his years in service is humble and penitent before his God.* Let the pagans celebrate the military victories. It's the Christian who knows, as one of our American admirals said when his men were cheering the sinking in flames of an enemy vessel: "Don't cheer, men. The poor devils are dying." He wasn't just being sentimental. He was saying in his own way what every truly Christian soldier feels. This business of war is a sinful business and there's nothing to cheer about, really. The best we can all do is repent of that which in each of us makes war possible and try in the future to live the sort of life that makes peace possible among men. The ancient prophet said: "What doth the Lord require of thee, but to do justly [and a Christian soldier may be an instrument of justice], and to love mercy [and he must always love mercy], and to walk humbly with thy God" (Mic. 6:8). Let others beat the drums; you remember to pray and pray the prayer of confession.

These are not easy days in which to live and anyone sells you short who tells you they are. These are not easy days in which to be young, because the sort of world we live in seems to make the young do most of the dirty work. These are not easy days in which to be a thinker, because there are no clear answers to the problems and we often get tired just thinking. These are not easy days in which to try to be a Christian, but try we must. I met a man the other day just back from Jerusalem. While there he had wanted to go to the Upper Room, the place where Jesus traditionally held the first Holy Communion with his disciples, giving them bread and wine. It wasn't easy to find and, when he got there, the door was barricaded with barbed wire. Two soldiers had to remove the roll of barbed wire before he could go in to pray.

It's a strange world, barbed wire and Holy Communion. As a Christian, you can't live just in a world of barbed wire and, as a Christian, you can't live in the world of Holy Communion either. But that's where a soldier becomes a soldier of the Cross. In the painful interior of your conscience you're going to have to put these two together.

TWENTY

When Death Strikes Your Family

AS SOME of you know, one of our senior students lost her father last week end. Death came, as it does so often to men in their prime, by sudden and unexpected heart attack. As a community our deepest sympathy and prayers go out to Mary and her family. And I should add that I was moved by what her roommates and friends here at college decided to do. Rather than send flowers to the funeral, they are giving money to the American Heart Foundation, which, through medical research, hopes some day to conquer this terrible disease. For college men and women that is a most intelligent and humane way to express their personal sympathy.

Of course, what happened to Mary happens to a number of us in each college class and in each college year. We might as well face it: death comes home to each of us on occasion. Otherwise we avoid it, and probably rightly so; we don't want to be morbid. But you can think about death without being morbid. Indeed that may be one good test of whether you're growing up. Philosophy probably starts when you face the brute fact "all men are mortal." And religion is probably born then, when you deal with the meaning of your finiteness. Here the boys are separated from the men and the adults from the children. Remember Willie Keith, the officer in Herman Wouk's *The Caine Mutiny?* One of the sailors had just given Willie a cigar; then the sailor went to his battle station on the ship. A bomb from a Kamikaze plane hit right at his station and blew him to bits. The novel continues: "With the smoke of the dead sailor's cigar wreathing around him, Willie passed to thinking about death and life and luck and God. Philosophers are at home with such thoughts, perhaps, but for other people it is actual torture when these concepts—not the words but the realities —break through the crust of daily occurrences and grip the soul. A half hour of such racking meditation can change the ways of a lifetime. Willie Keith crushing the stub in the ashtray was not the Willie who had lit the cigar. That boy was gone for good." Well, death, the reality of it, does change us: the boy is gone for good, or the girl, or the happy kid. College men and women who squirm out of it, or evade or laugh it off, are deceiving themselves. After all, the terrible truth is that we live in a century in which the young, the beautiful young, do as much dying as the old.

When death comes home to us, what do we, as intelligent Christians, do? We should face it, first of all, with a certain under-standing of ourselves and others. In other words, whether in class or out of it, we should comprehend the psychology of grief. For instance, as psychologists we know there's no point in trying to cover up sorrow or be unemotional or unexpressive. The good Lord never intended us to be only brave, simply cold and stoical. On the day of his wife's death, Fichte, the German philosopher, went to his university lecture room and gave his lecture the same as usual. No doubt it was a great demonstration of duty and will power and self-control, but most of us aren't made that way and it's just as well we aren't. Death is death, and there's no turning back from the loss of it. When Dad goes there's a hole in life, a big hole. As St. Augustine wrote about the death of a friend: "I could not see how the sun could shine when half of my soul lay dead." That's more like it. When half of your soul lies dead, don't try to cover up your sorrow. The study of psychology warns us all: grief that is unexpressed today, tomorrow may find false and neurotic expression.

And certainly psychology can help us understand some of the

morbid feelings we all have in the presence of death. Dr. Erich Lindemann of Harvard says, for instance, that most of us in sorrow develop excessive feelings of guilt. We accuse ourselves of having not been home when our loved one died; we should have been around to help. Yet probably all we were doing was carrying out the routine of life either at business or at school. But in grief we accuse ourselves, all of us. Or we are apt to say: "I should have treated him better. Why, the very week before he died I got mad at him and forgot to be kind. I wonder if I even hastened his death." These feelings are false and excessive, you see, but very common. And it's good to study psychology if only to know how common they are, for your own good and for the comfort of others.

But not only does psychology help us when death comes home or near to us and our friends; I think biology helps too. Biology is the science of life and you can't study life very long without realizing that "in the midst of life we are always in the midst of death." A freshman girl expressed it to a group of us the other night. She said: "If there were no death there would be no new ideas, no advances in civilization and culture. The old would just get older and dominate the race. Youth and newness would have no meaning." It's hard to improve on that statement. The biologist or botanist knows that the individual bud must die in order that new life may be born. And the sociologist knows that an old society becomes a feeble society. The life sciences deal continually with death, and their very objectivity can at times be a comfort to us. Look at the leaves of autumn, dying in a thousand colors and whirled away with the winds. And while persons are more than leaves, it is still true that without autumn there would probably be no spring, in nature or in human civilization.

But what of our religious faith: when death comes home to us what has that to say? Naturally we turn to the Bible. Death in the Bible is at times "the grim reaper." All our days "are like grass which groweth up. In the morning it flourisheth, and groweth up; in the evening it is cut down, and withereth" (Ps. 90:5–6). Or death is sometimes spoken of as sleep: in sleep you seem to move into a different world from that of waking; so death is a few winks of sleep and then you wake in a new world in "that undiscovered country from whose bourne no traveller returns." But the picture I like best in the Bible is in the 90th Psalm. Speaking of death the writer says: "So teach us to number our days, that we may apply our hearts unto wisdom" (Ps. 90:12). Rabbi Liebman, author of *Peace of Mind,* used to speak of "that great teacher death." That to me is the best picture in the Bible. Death is your greatest teacher.

According to Christianity, what does death teach? First of all, *death teaches that we haven't all the time in the world, no one of us.* "Teach us to number our days," says the Psalmist. John R. Mott, the great missionary statesman, puts it another way: "Next to God, respect time." Death teaches us to respect time, our little time.

This respect for time is, I suspect, seldom thought of when we're young. We like to think that we've got all the time in the world, plenty of time to learn and plenty of time to love and plenty of time to get started in a job. But actually that may be one of the illusions of youth. We have a lot of people in America who say in their twenties, "I've got all the time in the world," and then in their forties they're saying, "Time has run out; it's too late." Indeed the mathematics of life may be quite uncomfortable. We often sing: "Swift to its close ebbs out life's little day." Leslie Weatherhead of London once tried to measure the average human life in terms of the waking hours of one day. What time are you living at? If your day starts at 7:00 in the morning and ends at 11:00 at night, then if you're fifteen years of age it's 10:25 in the morning of your little life; if you're eighteen, it's already 11:00; if you're twenty-five, which is the time many of us finish our education, then it's already 12:42 in the afternoon. In other words, by the time you've finished your education, your preparation for life, the most any of us has is an afternoon and an evening in which to live to the glory of God and the service of our fellow men. Even for you young people, life, when you think of it mathematically, is quite a "little day," too little to waste much of it. So teach us, death, teach us to respect time, to number our days.

Furthermore, the thought of death and the experience of it in our families certainly teach us another lesson: that *some things in this mortal life are deathless and these are the values we must pursue and hold dear.* "Teach us to number our days," says the Psalm. Why? "That we may apply our hearts unto wisdom." The modern translation is "That we may obtain an understanding heart." Evidently for the Psalmist, the thought of death not only gave a certain urgency to life; it also helped him to make moral decisions. What is good in life is what death cannot quite touch, like wisdom, or an understanding heart, or love, or the service of man and God. Death teaches all of us to see and love the Eternal.

This is why Christians speak of death as a judgment. "Judgment" in the Greek means, simply, to discern, to see things in their true color. So the thought of death or its near presence should make most of us discern better, see life in its true color. As some of you know, my wife spent a year in the hospital in an iron lung. The first time we brought her home after that she kept looking at the house, with its furniture, its curtains, its books, and saying: "How cluttered up we are. We have so much stuff we don't need. We ought to simplify our living." At first I thought she was fooling but then I found out she meant it. It's inevitable: those who have been close to death must see life with different eyes from ours. What once was important must now seem so unimportant; what once we thought we possessed we now know we never possess; what once was our security becomes strangely insecure under the judgment of death. Death is the divine shock treatment, we have been told—by which I gather, that just as mental patients are sometimes shocked back into a sense of reality, so the thought of death strips away our securities of the past and shocks all of us into a new sense of reality, of what clutters up our living and what is lasting. As Jan Struthers once wrote of war: "That glorious, awful and eye-opening time." Death opens our eyes and helps us see what is mortal and immortal about us. Death is your great teacher. It gives you judgment. It gives you discernment.

But the Christian goes on and says something further: *death helps us all to see God more clearly.* We shall see him "face to face," we are told. This does not mean we face him in fear, like the crude ads on dangerous highway curves: "Prepare to meet thy God." No, we face him as the eternal home of our souls, dimly known on earth, but then someday better known. "Lord, thou hast been our dwelling place in all generations." So teach us, death— to come face to face with God.

Naturally, I don't know what the experience of death is like. I've watched some people die, though. And death is not a pretty sight. Let me read you Thomas Wolfe's description of a modern hospital: "Suddenly one got an image of his own death in such a place as this, and the image of that death was somehow shameful. It was an image of a death without man's ancient pains and old, gaunt aging—an image of death drugged and stupefied out of its ancient terror and stern dignities, of a shameful death that went out softly, dully in anaesthetized oblivion, with the fading smell of chemicals on a man's final breath." That's modern death: we are but dust.

But if most of us die that way, most of us die in faith, too, with quite a bit of expectation. You'll never see the human spirit rise so high as in the act of dying. I don't care what theology you have, most men see God more clearly when the ties of earth loosen their hold. And the mystery of death seems to be that we are more than fading chemicals, than anaesthetized oblivion; our spirits, says the Christian, are made for God and to their home they go. I just quoted Thomas Wolfe, the novelist; I shouldn't leave him there. He probably wouldn't call himself a Christian, but no greater statement of faith can be found than the Credo at the end of *You Can't Go Home Again*. "Something has spoken to me in the night, burning the tapers of the waning year. Something has spoken to me in the night, and told me I shall die, I know not where. Saying: To lose the earth you know, for greater knowing; to lose the life you have for greater life; to leave the friends you loved for greater loving; to find a land more kind than home, more large than earth—whereon the pillars of this earth are founded, toward which the conscience of the world is tending—a wind is rising and the rivers flow." As Christians we die in some such faith that life beyond will be better because we better see God.

One further word. Death teaches us that we haven't all the time in the world, that some things in this mortal life are quite deathless. Death helps us to see God more clearly and live by faith, "to lose the earth you know for greater knowing." But for the Christian *the thought of death always reminds us of the ultimate mystery of every person we meet in life.* People are really not young or old, not rich or poor: death does not pay much attention to such adjectives. Rather, as Jesus saw them, all men are eternal souls. These few years that we know each other are only the first part of a greater journey. In this very room, if we only had eyes to see, there are a million hours of immortality. So you can never look at men as merely students, or merely workers, or merely tools in an industrial machine, or merely fodder for the giant cannons of war. All men are really travelers, and death is but the beginning of a larger and longer journey. About every little one of us there is always a sense of mystery, of infinite destiny.

I hope we can learn to see each other that way, not in terms of the body, which soon becomes dust, but in terms of the soul and the things of the soul, which rise immortal out of our dust. Then you and I can reverence the mystery in each one of us, and face death, not without sorrow but equally not without hope. Artists tell us that one of the earliest designs man ever made was the design of the lotus. The tombs of Egypt are covered with myriads of little lotus buds with their opening faces and petals. For us Americans the nearest equivalent of the lotus is the water lily. Its roots are in the earth at the bottom of a pond; through the water it lifts a long but very fragile stem; finally it enters a third element, the air, and there it blossoms into infinite color and beauty. And these primitive artists dared to say the lotus is a picture of the soul of man. Born of earth, a thing of clay, the animal past, for a few years it grows among us as a thin fragile stem we call life, until one day it enters a new element and there in the sunlight of God blossoms into a beauty such as our eyes have never seen. So, teach us, death, to look with new wonder at the infinite beauty and mystery of each and every life around us.